**ADVANCE AGENTS OF AMERICAN DESTINY**

## Other Books by Roy F. Nichols

The Democratic Machine: 1850–1854

America Yesterday and Today
(with C. A. Beard and W. C. Bagley)

The Growth of American Democracy
(with Jeannette P. Nichols)

The Republic of the United States: A History
(with Jeannette P. Nichols)

A Short History of American Democracy
(with Jeannette P. Nichols)

Franklin Pierce

Disruption of the American Democracy

*William  Shaler*

# Advance Agents of American Destiny

*by*

Roy F. Nichols

Philadelphia
University of Pennsylvania Press

973
N621a
1956

*To*

*St. George L. Sioussat
friend of long standing*

# Acknowledgments

MY MOST grateful acknowledgment is made of the aid which the late Mrs. Gabrielle Shaler Webb generously gave to me. She made available to me the large and important collection of William Shaler manuscripts which she later deposited in the Historical Society of Pennsylvania. Her estate granted me permission to use the portrait of William Shaler. My thanks go, likewise, to her kinswoman, Mrs. Walton Craig Hill. Mrs. Natalia Summers, of the State Department, gave me much invaluable help as I was exploring the files in her charge. She had great capacity for cheering on the labors of those doing research. The late S. W. Boggs, Special Adviser on Geography of the State Department, and Mrs. Sophia A. Saucerman, Acting Special Adviser on Geography in the State Department, have afforded me valuable information. Dr. Ernest Gruening, recently Governor of Alaska, went to a great deal of trouble to furnish me with material for the last chapter. My colleagues, Professors Arthur C. Bining and Loren C. Eiseley, together with Dr. Henry P. Beers and Carl L. Lokke of the National Archives and Arnold K. Borden, supplied me with a good deal of bibliographical and statistical material. I am further indebted to Dr. Kent Roberts Greenfield, Chief of Military History, Department of the Army, and to his associate, Professor George F. Howe. Dr. John Kirtland Wright and Professor Samuel Flagg Bemis were helpful in the matter of maps. Through their courtesy, the American Geographical Society and Henry Holt and Company granted permission to use the maps. Miss Sarah E. Calhoun and

Mrs. Rose Marie Di Muro did wonders in transcribing my difficult handwriting. Portions of this book have appeared in *The Hispanic American Historical Review, The Pennsylvania Magazine of History and Biography, The New England Quarterly, The American Historical Review, The George Washington University Studies in Hispanic American Affairs,* and the *State Department Conference Series.* Acknowledgment is made to the editors of these publications for their interest. I am particularly happy to acknowledge the receipt of several timely grants from the Committee on the Advancement of Research of the University of Pennsylvania.

# Contents

# Illustrations and Maps

# Introduction

TODAY when the earth has shrunk into unbelievably small compass and distance has almost been annihilated, there is little left of the mystery of far-off, unknown places. In the late eighteenth century when the United States came into being it was far different, for then so much of the earth was still unknown. The erstwhile thirteen colonies were far from the center of world affairs in those days. Their knowledge of the globe and their interests outside of their own bounds were painfully narrow and circumscribed; but these limits were to be short-lived. The new republic was remarkably possessed of the power of growth, the desire to expand and the zeal for discovery. It was soon to look beyond its near horizons and in the end no corner of the earth was to be unsearched by its citizens.

The pioneers in this new phase of discovery had varied tasks. They must direct the adjustment which the former British colonists had thrust upon them by independence. As subjects of the mother country, they had been unaware of certain of the responsibilities of complete freedom. Such matters as diplomacy and the protection of commerce had been the Crown's concern, not theirs. When they no longer had the protection of the British flag and of British armed strength, they must build up a power and a prestige of their own. To this end a series of far-roving agents went forth to secure the enlargement of American interests.

With some, the prime objects were commercial or diplomatic. With others, the motive was a sublime curiosity, so much of the world was yet undiscovered in 1776. Most im-

11

portant and most dynamic, however, were those fired with the zeal for propaganda, men who were missionaries preaching the gospel of the new and enlightened republican way of life. Whatever the inspiration, they went forth on various missions, explored new horizons, brought back information and created new opportunities. The amount of the earth's surface covered by these people in the small barks to whose frailty they entrusted themselves is unbelievable.

As the years advanced and new interests succeeded one another in an age of steam and electricity and air travel, agents with similar zeal continued their search for opportunities in far places. Their activities and their enterprise have been notable even into our own day.

These advance agents of American destiny have been on the whole more or less obscure men, few of whom gained much fame from their efforts. In fact, most of them are scarcely referred to in the pages of the chronicles. Yet they deserve more of history than they have received. It was their labor and talent and particularly their adventurous enterprise that provided the entering wedges and only after their work was done could statesmen take up the task and receive whatever of renown—or opprobrium—was to be their lot.

Upon the pages that follow are set forth some of the exploits of certain of these far-venturing Americans. Their prowess illustrates various fundamental traits in the American character still essential to the continued maintenance of the way of free enterprise. It points out the origin of certain interests which in this present epoch have taken on a new significance to the United States as it awakes to new concepts of geography and to a new understanding of time and space.

Roy F. Nichols

March 3, 1956

ADVANCE AGENTS OF AMERICAN DESTINY

# 1. Along the Spanish Main

O NE day in mid-August, 1776, some battered flatboats were tied up to the levees at the Spanish port of New Orleans. An American, George Gibson, and some two dozen "traders" from way up river clambered ashore, weather-beaten and travel-weary. They might well be, for they had been floating for a month down the treacherous and blistering Mississippi. They had started from Pittsburgh July 19th, just a fortnight after the adoption of the Declaration of Independence, and had at length come to the end of a truly perilous journey.

These "traders" were not what they appeared to be. They were soldiers in disguise and their leader, Captain Gibson, was on a diplomatic mission. He had been sent by Governor Patrick Henry of Virginia and General Charles Lee to negotiate for aid from the Spanish Governor, Luis de Unzaga. These revolutionary leaders hoped that in return for help offered to Spain in regaining Florida, recently become a British colony, the New Orleans authorities might allow trade in war material for the benefit of the Patriot army. Gibson bore letters not only to the Governor but to a fellow Pennsylvanian, resident at New Orleans, Oliver Pollock. These two men were to inaugurate significant trends in American destiny.

One of the first needs which the United States, newly dedeclared independent, had that summer of 1776, was to create a new place for themselves in the world of commerce.

As British colonies they had been, officially at least, barred from trade with some of their nearest neighbors in potentially most profitable trading centers. The mercantile policy of the Crown had been designed to keep the colonies producers of raw material to be sold to Britain, and purchasers of processed goods procured almost wholly in British markets. The erstwhile colonies were now embarking upon a series of efforts to obtain commercial independence and the privilege of buying and selling where they would. Their first thoughts were turned to inaugurating trade with the nearest commercial marts, those of the West Indies.

The isles along the Spanish Main had ever been an invitation to the enterprising among the inhabitants of the nearby continent. From the first years of the thirteen colonies, adventurous and curious mariners sought profit from these isles; occasionally visitors frequented such pleasant places in search of milder climate. Small wonder was it then, that when the American Revolution burst forth, these islands were objects of immediate Patriot interest. The new republic desired their aid and sent resourceful agents to secure it. These newcomers were the first to seek a measure of "hemispheric solidarity."

The Continental Congress hoped to find these island colonies co-operative and useful, for they possessed markets and stores where the Patriots might obtain supplies, and where revolutionary privateers might find refuge. Congressional committees and state agencies, therefore, dispatched agents to the French, Dutch and Spanish ports in the West Indies and to other ports on the continent to establish business and quasi-diplomatic arrangements in them with their rulers and their merchants. This was not difficult with the French and Dutch islands but the task of penetrating the barriers surrounding the Spanish American empire was long and tortuous and enlisted the services of emissaries of a wide variety of talents and interests.

Spain had always endeavored to keep all save Spaniards from access to her colonies. Consequently, they had been a tempting field of adventure for British colonial seamen, made all the more alluring by Spain's attempts to keep others out. Illicit trade had flourished and tales of sea fights, not only with Spanish *guarda costa* but more particularly with buccaneers, were told with gusto. During the several wars of the eighteenth century in which the British colonies had been involved, these Spanish islands had seen many a Yankee trader and privateer, to the mutual profit of islander and visitor. The brief British occupation of Havana in 1762–1763 had been a field day and when Great Britain acquired Florida, trading ventures secured a convenient operating base. The old barriers were down, particularly as Spain did not build them up when she took over New Orleans and Louisiana as compensation for the loss of Florida. The Patriots were not blind to the fact that Spain resented the loss of Florida, and hope flourished that the Spanish government might be interested in extending credit and supplies in return for help in driving the British out of their recent capture. Hence Gibson's mission to the nearest possible favorable Spanish market.

The adventurous captain was a Pennsylvanian born in Lancaster who as a boy had come to Philadelphia to learn to be a merchant. He had been an apprentice at the metropolis and had gone to the West Indies on various trading vessels as agent of the owners. He had later engaged in Indian trading in the Ohio Valley and when the Revolution broke out he had become captain of a company which for a time was stationed at the capital of Virginia. His experience, an unusual language equipment, and his mercantile connections commended him to Henry and to Lee. So they sent him south with letters to Pollock whom he may have known in earlier days in Philadelphia. At least, they had mutual mercantile acquaintances.

The man with whom Gibson was to join forces in New Orleans, Oliver Pollock, was an Irishman who had migrated to Pennsylvania in 1760 and thence within two years had departed for the West Indies. It was the psychological moment, for the British had just captured Havana and were opening trade opportunities. Pollock settled in this ancient city and through Catholic connections gained the friendship of certain Spanish officials, notably General Alejandro de O'Reilly. When Havana was closed after its return to the Spaniards in 1763, he transferred his business to New Orleans now under Spanish rule, and as O'Reilly soon became governor, he prospered under the latter's patronage. In the meantime, he had maintained valuable Philadelphia connections, notably with those leading merchants, Robert Morris and Thomas Willing, whose interests seemed to know no bounds. Like a good Irishman, he was sympathetic with the efforts of the thirteen colonies to free themselves from the British yoke and he had already done something for the cause. In April, 1776, he had been influential in securing permission for several Patriot vessels to take refuge at New Orleans from British pursuers.

Gibson's mission had a peculiar but unmistakable success, largely through Pollock's shrewd capacity to use influence. In typically Spanish fashion, the captain and his men were quite publicly arrested and thrown into jail. In the meantime, he was secretly permitted to purchase gunpowder which was shipped up the river. Then Gibson was oh-so-carelessly allowed to escape and go after the powder. Pollock in the meantime rejoiced in new business opportunities as he proceeded to act as Virginia's agent in further transactions. His ambition soared and he offered his services to Congress in a like capacity. Official Spanish policy was providing attractive side speculations for such an agent. The King of Spain had decided to join the French in secret loans to American agents in Europe, so he sent orders to New Orleans and Havana permitting co-operation with the colonials. A new governor, Bernardo de Galvez, nephew of the powerful Joseph de Galvez, Minister of the Indies, resident of Madrid, was ordered to New Orleans. When he arrived, zealous for the recapture of Florida, Oliver Pollock fed his enthusiasm and in May, 1777, the American wrote to Congress that his efforts were proving fruitful. He requested authority to enlist troops and aid Galvez.

Even before they received this last report, the Committee on Commerce of Congress had been impressed with Pollock's interest, and on June 12, 1777, had appointed him their agent. The delivery of his commission was delayed and it was not until the following March that Pollock received it. The means of its delivery were supplied by the increasing interest of Spain in the Patriot's success. The Spanish firm of Joseph Gardoqui and Sons of Bilbao had begun the shipment of supplies for the Americans via New Orleans, and Captain James Willing, for the firm of Morris and Willing, had been sent down the Mississippi by the Commerce Committee of Congress to take charge of these munitions. He bore Pollock's commission with him. On his way he caused quite a stir by capturing Natchez and seizing British vessels which he sold as prizes at New Orleans. Upon his arrival, Pollock received the delayed commission as a full-fledged agent and set himself whole-heartedly to aid de Galvez in the capture of Mobile and Pensacola and to finance George Rogers Clark in the conquest of the North-west.

## II

While de Galvez and Pollock were working out plans for co-operation in the Floridas and in the Mississippi region, at New Orleans, greater interest was developing at the real seat of authority, Havana. Here the Captain-General, Mar-ques de la Torre, ruled with almost absolute authority as he was possessed of wide discretionary powers. He had been watching as closely as he could the course of events. Not only had he sent over an agent, Miguel Eduardo, to New Orleans in May, 1776, but early in 1777 he had sent others to Port-au-Prince, Jamaica, and to St. Augustine. Just as de la Torre was succeeded by Diego José Navarro as Cap-tain-General, Juan de Miralles was dispatched to make con-tact with General Washington and Congress, a step ordered from Madrid in August, 1777.

Miralles was a Havana merchant, connected with the family of Eligio de la Puente, a slave-trading interest, and with the firm Aguírre, Aristegui y Cía, of Cadiz who had extensive dealings with the British isles and the American colonies. He had been much engaged in contraband trade with the mainland colonies when Cuba was supposed to be closed to such traffic. In fact, he knew his way around and was now much interested in the success of the Revolution because of the trading opportunities which it would open. In the meantime, he was alert for chances of profit through traffic in supplies. His journey was to be as much a trade-promotion tour for his personal benefit as it was a diplo-matic mission.

Miralles left Havana, December 31, 1777, and landed at Charleston, South Carolina, on January 9th. Here he be-

gan at once on commerce and diplomacy. As it was necessary to send back reports to Havana at frequent intervals
he appointed a Charleston merchant, George Abbot Hall,
as dispatch bearer and gave him a permit to ship a cargo
for trading purposes at Havana whenever he carried dispatches. Miralles himself bought a ship from Hall and sent
back a cargo of rice which the Havana authorities were to
take in return for sugar which they sent Miralles for sale.
The Cuban agent fraternized with the Patriots, attended
their social gatherings and made himself *persona grata.*
It was all going to be good for Cuban business so long hampered by the old restrictions.

Miralles remained in Charleston until he learned of the
arrival of Gerard, the first French envoy to Philadelphia.
Then he began a leisurely journey northward, punctuated
by a sojourn with Governor Patrick Henry of Virginia who
was negotiating with de Galvez and Pollock at New Orleans.
About July 1, 1778, the Cuban arrived in Philadelphia and
was soon busy in promoting trade. Here likewise it was
necessary to secure dispatch bearers, so he arranged for a
packet service to Havana which would also serve for trading purposes. He associated himself with Robert Morris,
as was to be expected, and stimulated in that merchant an
appetite for Cuban trade which was to grow. Miralles hired
vessels at intervals from Morris to carry his dispatches and
most of these boats were loaded with sugar, hides, wine,
coffee, and other goods. As time went on, Morris secured
permission to send ventures of his own in tar and lumber in
return for reducing the charter rate on his ships.

Despite this progress, trading with Cuba was still difficult,
not only because of Spanish restrictions but also because
of the hampering effect of American regulations. Congress
had been experiencing a great deal of difficulty in feed-

ing the army. The only money which Congress could command was its homemade paper and this the farmers were increasingly reluctant to take. It was more profitable to export their foodstuffs to the West Indies for hard money. So since June, 1776, Congress and the state legislatures had imposed various embargoes to keep food at home for the army. At first these prohibitions were haphazard and generally applied to meat. But bad harvests caused a more drastic enactment in June, 1778, which forbade export of wheat, rice, rye, Indian corn, flour and bread. Such an embargo ruined many plans including those of Miralles to send down flour to Havana, where a ready market was waiting. The Cuban, therefore, urged his government to open its ports to trade, an action which he believed would encourage Congress to lift the embargo.

Spain's decision to enter the war against England, proclaimed in June, 1779, bettered this situation. Miralles was authorized to start negotiations for joint military operations against Florida, and in the Southwest de Galvez and Pollock could co-operate even more effectively. Trade opportunities opened up likewise, for the British soon cut off Spain from her colonies and if they were to receive the supplies they needed, they must seek them elsewhere. Spain bowed to the inevitable and on October 12, 1779, issued an order allowing Cubans to buy provisions and sell produce to the revolting colonies. No manufactured goods, however, might enter this trade. When this order reached Cuba, the Captain-General, Navarro, wrote to Miralles to send flour, rice, meat, tar, pitch and masts, and authorized him to seek permission from Congress for these exports. This opportunity was particularly welcome to Cubans because they were suffering from too large a surplus of sugar which they now might expect to export in exchange.

## III

Miralles was destined never to receive this welcome news for while visiting General Washington at Morristown he had died, April 28, 1780. The Captain-General's order therefore, came into the hands of Miralles' secretary, Francisco Rendon. He lacked any power to act so he went to the French Minister Luzerne who through Morris obtained the necessary export permission. Congress recommended that the state of Maryland permit the sale of 3000 barrels of flour. Rendon and Luzerne agreed that it would be wiser not to publish the news that Cuban ports were open as this might encourage violation of the embargo. Instead, they informed a few of their friends among the merchants and arranged with them to supply the flour, through Robert Morris and John Dorsey of Baltimore, a nice little inside job.

This contract for 3000 barrels proved difficult to fill, for flour was scarce. Morris and his associates had to pick it up at various places and send it in many ships. Permission had to be sought to get some of it from the Dutch island of St. Eustatius in the West Indies. It was evident that an agent was necessary, so Robert Morris hired Robert Smith of Baltimore, recently a captain of dragoons, and sent him to Havana, August 17, 1780, to act for him.

Trade began to expand. Rendon reported that Philadelphia had beef, pork, lard and other food for sale, even live cattle, and that its merchants wanted sugar, molasses and "strong waters." Morris planned to invest the proceeds of the flour sales in sugar. Havana, therefore, began buying these commodities and rice, fish, butter, tar and lumber as well, while American merchants added coffee and hides to their purchases. Besides Morris and Dorsey, Matthew Irwin and Company, and Lacare and Mallet of Philadelphia, there was competition from Wilmington. Delaware repealed her embargo and the firm of Mead and Company offered to carry dispatches free. So this firm, through its supercargo, Samuel Wilcocks, did a thriving business.

Still the trade was subject to numerous difficulties. Duties were high in Cuban ports, ranging around thirty per cent import and ten per cent export, sometimes augmented by other taxes. Americans could not do business directly but only through some Cuban business man. Ships were often detained while military or naval preparations were being made, so that no word of what was going might leak out. These delays in the hot climate often caused cargoes to spoil and their owners to lose heavily. Morris himself was not too fortunate, as he lost three ships which were captured or wrecked. Likewise, he was accused of breaking his contract because his agent ordered the vessels carrying dispatches to make stops at various West Indian ports instead of proceeding directly to Philadelphia. The Wilmington merchants were gaining in the competition.

By March, 1781, Rendon could report that trade was constantly growing. Forty thousand quintals of flour had been carried direct from American ports, not counting that which had been taken from St. Eustatius. Also, the recent capture of that port, February 3, 1781, had increased the direct trade between Cuba and the United States. Then came a blow. The proximity of the British and French fleets that winter worried the Captain-General, Diego José Navarro. Vessels going to and from Cuba might be too easily captured. Heretofore, in times of such danger, he had closed the port of

Havana temporarily, now he repeated this order with seemingly greater determination.

## IV

This embargo led Smith to report to his employer the desirability of new arrangements. He suggested that some of the long detentions and the heavy attendant expenses might be prevented if some American were vested with an official capacity. He offered to assume such responsibility if Congress authorized it. Morris, enjoying a new position of influence since April 30th when he had been appointed superintendent of finance, made an official recommendation. He assured Congress that if Smith were granted a commission as "Consul, Resident or Agent" at the port of Havana such action would be useful to trade in general "and particularly so to some Operations I have now in view for the Publick Service." Congress agreed almost immediately, electing Smith, June 27th, as agent at Havana to act under the orders of the Superintendent of Finance or of Congress.*

Morris did not forget that Smith could perform for him other duties than those involved in looking for trade. Morris had a plan for a national bank, the Bank of North America to be, but he lacked hard money to use as capital. He hoped to obtain it by selling to the Captain-General of Cuba some bills of exchange which the French government had authorized him to draw. This negotiation he planned to entrust to Smith and also he hoped he might sell some of the bank

* Two other attempts to establish agents had been made at Havana. In the spring of 1778, Pollock had sought the Captain-General's permission to set up in Havana an agent of the United States to receive vessels and sell prizes. Also in April, 1781, North Carolina had attempted to establish Spyers Singleton there as the state's agent. Both of these requests Navarro had denied.

stock in Havana. Unfortunately, the warship that bore these letters was captured by the British and the letters and bills, in the meantime, were thrown overboard to prevent their seizure.

Smith presented his commission to the Captain-General but the latter was no more ready to receive him than he had been to recognize Pollock or Singleton. He was polite but firm in his statement that he had no power to receive an agent. Smith remained, nevertheless, and reported a second plan. He wished to establish a prize court at Havana and he requested that he be given authority to issue commissions to privateers and that Congress gain permission from Madrid to send prizes into Havana. Such power Congress was unwilling to grant.

Robert Livingston, Secretary of Foreign Affairs, wrote Smith that he must content himself with acting as observer. He was to send reports to Philadelphia regularly regarding military operations and concerning commerce, husbandry, revenue and the condition of the people in general. In the meantime, Livingston through John Jay, American representative at Madrid, sought to gain larger trade privileges in the West Indies and on the Mississippi. He wrote Jay, "The Havana trade, notwithstanding the important advantages it affords to Spain, meets with the most unjustifiable interruptions. Vessels have been detained for months together in order to carry on the expeditions which Spain has formed, no adequate satisfactions being allowed for them, and then sent away without convoy, by which means many of them have fallen into the hands of the enemy."

This situation had been intensified by the great victory of Admiral Rodney over the French fleet off the Saints in April. Havana was tight shut and Smith could do nothing. Some sixty captains were watching their vessels tied up at the wharves. Fortunately, Oliver Pollock stopped at Havana on his way to the United States. He convinced the Captain-General that such a policy was cutting off supplies that de Galvez needed for an expedition he was planning against Jamaica, and again the embargo was lifted.

After Pollock left, Smith turned to what proved to be his last task. Morris was making another attempt to secure specie from the Captain-General. He sent bills down by the *Alliance* in the summer but that ship was pursued by British vessels and driven back to port. Not until November did Morris succeed in sending his bills to Havana. Then it developed that Smith was unable to interest the authorities in such a proposition. They would not buy this exchange. In the spring Smith died, leaving American commerce in a precarious state.

This unfortunate end of Smith's misison made the selection of a new agent imperative. As Seagrove, "a worthy American merchant," reported to Morris, "An officer appointed by Congress becomes more and more necessary everyday. [There is] daily abuse of our Flag by other nations in introducing cargoes here, our Flag having indulgencies that no other has, but unless there is a stop put to this, we shall lose all character and indeed have the port shut against us. Ten or twelve arrive in a week from St. Thomas's with provisions, dry goods, negroes, etc. and are guilty of every irregularity with intention to bring the Americano into disrepute. Was there an Agent or Consul here, all this might be prevented. It is a matter that calls for redress." Congress thought so too and elected Oliver Pollock to this post, May 27, 1783. He had been effective in New Orleans and recently his friend Bernardo de Galvez had been made Captain-General of Cuba. It seemed an auspicious appointment. But almost as it was made, its effectiveness was cancelled. Spain had ordered colonial ports to be closed under date of August 29, 1782, believing the war to be about over and just recently the Captain-General had set himself to obey. On May 30, 1783, he ordered Spanish-American ports under his jurisdiction firmly barred to all save Spanish ships.

All unconscious of this new move, Pollock had loaded two vessels with merchandise and departed for Havana to combine diplomacy with his own profit. To his dismay, he found Havana closed under the new order, and worse still, his friend, de Galvez, had not arrived. He was permitted to enter with no great cordiality, only to find that business opportunities were no longer possible. Little success attended his efforts to exercise official functions to aid Americans and he was beset by his creditors. The United States had not reimbursed him for the money he had borrowed at New Orleans on his own security, and now that Pollock was within Spanish jurisdiction, his property was attached, he was accused of smuggling, and even when all foreigners were expelled from Cuba in February, 1784, he was detained until his debts should be paid. He had to wait a year until his friend, de Galvez, arrived, before he was permitted to leave. In this interval, the trade which had been so flourishing all but disappeared. The dawn of peace and the decline of trade removed the need of agents and incidentally destroyed the hope of profits for themselves, the feature which had attracted them to service. Not until another plague of war visited the world did adventurous American agents again attempt to set themselves up along the Spanish Main.

# 2. Further Hispanic Frustration

## I

THE wars which followed close on the heels of the French Revolution revived the hopes which the United States merchants cherished of opening rich trade with the Spanish colonies and the determination of the State Department to establish agents in those tempting ports. As Napoleon was beginning his meteoric rise to fame, Secretary Timothy Pickering set his hand and seal to a commission for Daniel Hawley of New York who under date of December 29, 1797 was designated consul at Havana. A long train of events had been leading up to this new attempt to establish an agent on the Spanish Main.

The position of the United States as an independent nation brought new problems in foreign trade which emphasized the need for diplomatic agents. The merchants of the new republic were now excluded from markets which they had enjoyed when they carried the British flag. Also, as there was peace, they could no longer carry on the profitable privateering which they had enjoyed at the expense of British shippers. Therefore the need of new markets became more imperative, and adventurous American captains began to seek entrance to ports as distant as those of South America and Asia. Particular interest developed in those nearest at hand, particularly those of the Spanish West Indies, so tempting and yet officially so tightly closed.

In the course of the growth of this venture, private enterprise and government promoted the creation of a consular system. With almost incredible slowness, Congress and the State Department organized such a service. As early as 1778 Congress had begun appointing consuls to French European ports under the treaty of alliance of that year, but it was not until 1790 that any effort was made to appoint such officials in the Western Hemisphere. Secretary Jefferson had dispatched them to French and Dutch West India ports but Congress refused any salaries, so these agents could only expect such "accidental advantages" as their titles might open to them. Under the simple rules drafted by Jefferson they could wear a uniform and the Secretary expected them to report on any preparations for war which they might observe.

Under such arrangements consuls did not fare very well. They found their West Indian experience anything but attractive. The local authorities in Haiti and Martinique did not want to recognize the consuls because they would thereby lose some fees as arranged under the consular treaty with France. Thus they were ignored during interminable delays. Also because no law had been passed, ship captains disregarded them. They would not file papers with them nor give them the information which the State Department wished. Only unfortunate sailors came to them for financial help and a passage home. Their efforts to persuade captains to take such sailors were frequently "treated with contempt and sometimes insult." Worst of all from the consuls' viewpoint, they did not find their position a help to their business operations.

Some had expected to go into lucrative commission business and one of them at least sent around circulars announcing his appointment and stating that he was establishing himself, at Cap François or elsewhere, "for the exclusive purpose of transacting commission business from this country, [and hoped] by reasonable charges, attention, and fidelity, to merit the confidence of those who may please favour him with their commands." However he found that it was not the custom of consuls in French ports to do business and Americans, therefore, took their business elsewhere. Likewise local officials had their peculiar schemes of graft and imposition. Under such conditions, these consuls soon became discouraged and returned home.

Finally Congress undertook to legislate and in 1792 formally established a consular system. The consuls were given regular powers to take depositions and to validate them with a seal which was to be recognized by the courts. They were to conserve the estates of American citizens who died within their jurisdiction. Likewise, they were to salvage wrecked ships and cargoes, and to see to it that shipmasters did not leave sailors stranded. A regular schedule of fees was established for these services and the officers were required to give bond. Under this act, further attempts were made to establish consulates in the French, Dutch and Danish possessions. There was no attempt to establish consular relations with the British Isles because of the refusal of the home government to tolerate them even clandestinely.

Curiously enough opportunities developed quite unexpectedly, and in typically Hispanic fashion, in the Spanish colonies. Spain's closure effected in 1784 was relaxed even before the outbreak of the next wars, in fact it lasted barely five years. Colonial needs were insistent and caused Spain to make concessions. Cuban sugar plantations were short of labor and on February 28, 1789, an order was issued permitting the entry of foreign vessels bringing Negro slaves. This exception was an invitation to contraband trade, because slave traders might well have other goods beneath their hatches and seemed to find no difficulty in landing them. Hamilton's first treasury report on trade in 1790 showed that there was a trade of some small proportion with the Spanish West Indies.

This wedge was driven deeper by the war resulting from the French Revolution which encouraged trade between the United States and Cuba. When Spain joined the monarchial allies against republican France in 1793, French privateers soon crippled Spanish commerce and Spanish America had to shift for itself. The then Captain-General of Cuba, Don Luis de Las Casas, was more enterprising than some of his predecessors. He sought to promote Cuban prosperity by admitting United States trade and thereby to avoid some of the cumbering expense of the clumsy intra-imperial exchange regulations. Besides, as in 1779, Cuba had accumulated a great surplus of sugar and the want of an outlet had produced an unendurable depth of depression which had been cumulating since 1785. Las Casas, therefore, used discretionary power and opened Cuban ports to trade in food with the United States, February 23, 1793. Four months later the urgencies of war caused Spain to issue a general order to this effect. Cuba could not be allowed to starve.

The relaxation of restrictions was not going to provide the freest sort of trade. British and French privateers preyed upon the shipping of the United States and Spanish officials levied tribute. Gardoqui, formerly representative of Spain at the seat of the new government of the United States, who was now Minister of Finance and Director of Commerce, had ideas of his own. He told William Short, the United States chargé at Madrid, that no trade was to be permitted and then proceeded to organize a peculiarly Spanish system. Josef de Jaudenes and Josef Ignacio de Viar, who had succeeded Gardoqui at Philadelphia as Spanish *encargados* or chargés on a joint commission of "equivocal and indefinite character," were now commissioned to promote trade, and in September, 1794, and the months following, Jaudenes established an enlarged consular system with Viar as consul-general resident in Philadelphia and seven consuls and vice consuls in the various ports. Under this system all merchants who wished to send food to Cuba must buy permits from Jaudenes directly or through the consuls. The fees paid for these permits went to Jaudenes and were shared with Viar and with any consul who had introduced the merchant in question; rumor had it that the fees were further shared with the wily Gardoqui himself. In the case of flour, the fees varied from one to three dollars a barrel, and as that commodity marketed in the United States at from six to ten dollars it was a heavy charge. Cuban authorities, too, were not very hospitable and found many exasperating ways to plague those who had purchased the permits.

For in spite of its concessions Spain was no more friendly to United States trade than before. Republican ideas were feared too strongly by colonial authorities and they would not grant any permanent privileges. Not only did the treaty of 1795 with the United States utterly ignore the question, but when Spain withdrew from the war that same year one of the first acts of peace was an order closing the ports. Jaudenes delayed the cessation of his profitable enterprise of permits as long as he could but he was shortly recalled and Viar gave a proclamation to the press dated June 12th suspending the trade and declaring the permits no longer valid. Within a month trade with Cuba was dead. But it was not to remain so long, for Spain's enjoyment of peace was brief. It was soon to be necessary to establish consulates, in spite of Spain's open hostility to this move.

Spain re-entered the war in 1796 as the ally of France.

With the new declaration of war, it was of course necessary for Cuba to depend once more upon the United States; and as soon as word came to Philadelphia in the fall of 1796, the new Spanish minister, the Marqués of Casa-Yrujo, started trade. The Spanish government, however, was quick to inform him that Jaudenes' permit system was not to be revived. Instead, Spain intended to resort to the monopoly system so hallowed by long abuse. The provisions needed by Cuba were to be supplied by Count Jaruco who was to reap the profit, presumably, in no small amount. As the count would not think of managing any commercial enterprise, he must choose an agent and for this purpose he commissioned Josef María de Yznardi, United States consul at Cadiz. Yznardi came to the United States to organize the monopoly and advertised in the United States press that trade must pass through his hands. Yznardi, not Yrujo, was to control the trade and Yrujo was in no way pleased. It was not long, however, before trade outgrew Jaruco's monopoly. The British navy was too much for Spain and France combined and Spain was soon cut off from its entire American empire. The result of this isolation was a sweeping order of November 18, 1797, throwing open not only Cuba but also all of Spain's American Atlantic ports. Within a year, the high levels of trade of the preceding period were doubled. The United States mercantile interests bade fair to reap a rich harvest from these new opportunities, as the American republic was the only convenient neutral with a sizable merchant marine, and the result was a practical monopoly. But the merchants were not to enjoy the good fortune unmolested, for France was a menace.

France was bent on crippling United States commerce in the West Indies. The French government resented the refusal of the Washington government to aid and was angry over the Jay treaty with France's enemy, Great Britain. Both France and Spain were certain that the United States policy was aiding England in her war against them; and Spain further feared that United States territory might be used as a base by Great Britain for attacks on Louisiana and Florida. France and Spain, therefore, by means of privateers preyed upon United States commerce in the Caribbean, on the pretext that most of it was bound for British island ports with contraband. By January, 1797, it was reported that Spain had captured and condemned thirty United States vessels in that region. Not only were these captures frequently made in Spanish territorial waters by its own ships but also by French vessels and, further, both flags used Spanish ports as convenient markets in which to sell the prizes. The crews of these prizes fared badly, for they landed frequently in Cuban or other West Indian ports, destitute and forced to shift for themselves. In this condition, United States seamen often became victims of tropical diseases and, strangers in strange and none too friendly lands, were robbed, maltreated and sometimes killed in water-front brawls. Measures must be taken to defend United States rights and interests in the Spanish colonies.

Heretofore, the United States government had been able to do little to protect its commerce and less to promote it. Jefferson and Randolph, as Secretaries of State, had recorded in their instructions to United States representatives in Madrid their desire to obtain commercial concessions in Spanish America by treaty, but saw no hope. Pinckney had endeavored to incorporate concessions in the treaty of 1795 to no avail. Pickering, when he entered the State Department, was more emphatic in his instructions and more interested as a New Englander than his Virginia predecessors had been, but all to no result. The increasing depredations now urged him to more decided action than note-writing, and he determined to take the bull by the horns. Consuls or agents for seamen and commerce, such as Smith and Pollock, were necessary in Spanish-American ports, not only to collect evidence of violations of neutral rights, but also to protest and to demand redress on the spot and to look after destitute seamen.

The events of 1797 persuaded Adams and Pickering to attempt to extend the embryo consular system to the Spanish colonies. The first move had been made in March just as Washington was retiring when Procopio Jacinto Pollock of Pennsylvania, probably a son of Oliver, was commissioned to New Orleans. In May, Pickering decided to try to establish an agent in Cuba. Spain would not of course officially recognize consuls in its American ports but Pickering was not without expedients. When Yznardi arrived in the United States on Jaruco's business, Pickering decided to use him. He was about to go to Cuba and as he was a consul recognized by Spain, though in a European port, why could not he look after United States interests while he was in Havana? Pickering so instructed him and he spent three months in Cuba. His errand, however, did not permit of a long stay and his efforts were not sufficient to improve conditions materially. In the meantime, further evidence of need caused Pickering to take other steps. It had been reported to him that the French were represented by a consul who, though not officially recognized, was permitted to remain. Under these circumstances, Daniel Hawley of New York was designated consul at Havana in December, 1797, and in the following June, Josiah Blakely of New York was appointed to the same office at Santiago. Yrujo immediately protested, pointing out that Spain recognized no consuls in its American possessions, not even those of its

French ally and he warned the Spanish ministry that the United States was attempting to worm its way into the colonies by this device. Hawley, nevertheless, was permitted to remain and to function after a fashion without recognition.

## II

Conditions did not improve and 1798 saw the United States in an angry mood. Napoleon had refused to receive American envoys unless they accepted the humiliation of paying bribes for the privilege. Spurred on by this insult Congress increased armament and passed a law in June forbidding all trade with France or its possessions. France on her part increased privateering operations and Spain as usual placed her ports at France's disposal. War seemed imminent, the navy was dispatched to the West Indies, and merchantmen were armed. At least two warships were commissioned to visit Caribbean ports and to take away destitute seamen. Others served as convoys to trading ships. In this crisis, Hawley was not a success. His chief interest was the enhancing of his own fortunes and he spent more of his time in getting trade permits and taking advantage of his fellow men than in looking after United States interests or seamen. Finally, in the winter of 1798–1799, he took a prolonged leave of absence from his post. At first, Pickering contented himself with sending Yznardi back to Havana, this time to establish a hospital for sailors. Then charges of sharp practice in prize cases made against Hawley were brought to the Secretary's attention. The consul had endeavored to cheat the owners and their insurance brokers. He had secured the release of a vessel brought in by a French privateer and instead of sending the ship to its destination, had sold the cargo and refused to turn over the proceeds. Furthermore, he tried to manufacture evidence in his favor. The consul was removed June 28, 1799.

A second trial was to be made immediately. On the next day, Hawley's successor was commissioned. A group of influential New York and Philadelphia business men and politicians joined in recommending John Morton, brother of the prominent Federalist, Colonel Jacob Morton, who also had another brother, George C. Morton, in business in Havana. John Morton was sent to Havana bearing a vigorous letter to the Captain-General demanding that the commerce of the United States be better protected from French privateers. Pickering was further hopeful that Morton might aid in stamping out an abuse. Because ships bearing slaves for sale were less liable to annoyance in Cuban ports and were more readily admitted, a trade in Negroes from the United States had developed. A law had been enacted in 1794 to prohibit their export but it was commonly violated. Morton was instructed to collect evidence. The new consul was a competent business man who had friends in Havana and was properly introduced by Yznardi, who acted as his interpreter while he was learning Spanish. The Captain-General received him unofficially and courteously, even referring a dispute between two Americans to him, but there was not the slightest sign of official recognition. Spain was adamant.

Spain, moreover, had repented of its enforced liberality in trade concessions and just as Morton was leaving for his post in August, 1799, word came which at first seemed a deathblow to United States trade. Spanish merchants, backed by their correspondents in Havana and Veru Cruz, had been working against the order of 1797. Cuban planters and some Havana merchants had profited much by the wartime freedom but their influence was unavailing; the Spanish interests were closer to the ministry. The United States minister reported that French influence, too, was pressing upon Spain to keep Americans out of West Indian ports. The adverse influence won, and on April 18, 1799, a peremptory royal order closed all Spain's American Atlantic ports. But it was not to be as bad as it seemed; Spanish regulations seldom were. The United States minister was assured that the purpose of the order was to keep out British trade, for the neutral merchants from the north of Europe were sending cargoes of British wares and the prohibition was directed against British manufacturers, not United States flour. Orders had been sent to permit the importation of provisions whenever it should be necessary. This report was confirmed by Morton from Havana and his reassuring letters to the collectors of ports were published in the press. Beyond causing temporary caution on the part of some shippers and serving as an excuse for seizures in the La Plata ports by Spanish officialdom, the edict had little discernible effect; and in the meantime circumstances were conspiring to cause another boom in United States trade with Spanish America.

Nelson had clipped the wings of French naval power by the destruction of the fleet at Aboukir Bay and when Napoleon got well settled in power after the coup d'état of 1799, and discovered American naval power, he started a new policy. The naval strength of the United States as early as February, 1799, was forty war vessels and 300 armed traders in the Caribbean, and two significant naval victories were achieved in the course of the next few months when the *Constellation* battled *L'Insurgente* and *La Vengeance*. French privateering was no longer profitable or even safe and Napoleon began to consider a treaty. By June, 1800, Morton could record that the coast of Cuba had not seen a French vessel for several months. So peaceful were the affairs that the consul took a prolonged leave in the fall of 1800, leaving his brother George C. Morton in charge. Next spring the latter reported:

> I observe with satisfaction that the general disposition of the Civil Department is to render justice and protect the rights and persons in an equal if not greater degree than those of their own, and the attention of the Marine Department is not to be exceeded, scarcely equalled by any nation. The wealth and importance of this colony has increased during the few years that it has been open to the American trade in a most astonishing degree, with regard to the habits of industry, knowledge of commerce, general civilization and comforts of life, and for the continuance of which trade after peace shall take place, many petitions have gone forward to court.

Trade increase was not confined to Cuba but extended to South America, not only on the Atlantic coast but also on the Pacific shores, to the great distress of the Spanish government which wished to consider that great ocean a *mare clausum*. Augustine Madan was commissioned consul at La Guaira, Venezuela, January 8, 1800, the first consul to be appointed to South America. Between 1798 and 1801, trade between the United States and Spanish America again nearly doubled.

Once again peace interrupted prosperity. In October, 1801, hostilities were concluded and Spanish commerce was again free from danger. When Consul Morton returned to Havana in December after a year's absence he found conditions becoming impossible. Peace had called forth the latent hostility to United States trade, at which need alone had caused the Spanish to wink. Don Luís de Viguri, the Intendant, seemed to have been the embodiment of this unfriendliness, as his actions showed. He had protested against the Captain-General's courtesy to Morton. He had arrested and imprisoned Consul Blakely at Santiago on a charge of smuggling. He had imposed arbitrary rules upon United States shippers without warning and connived at clandestine trade with the British, permitting the latter to sell in Cuba many of the cargoes captured from Americans. The Intendant also, so Morton reported, was not above taking "presents" and the pleasantly disposed Captain-General maintained that he had no control over him. Morton succeeded in obtaining Blakely's release and set about winding up his affairs, for the Federalists were out of power and Jefferson was about to appoint Robert Young of the District of Columbia as Morton's successor.

### III

No sooner had the official confirmation of the peace arrived, two days before Christmas, 1801, than the Captain-General and the Intendant hurried, quite in contrast to their usual pace, to revive the prohibitions under their discretionary power. Without warning, the ports were closed on Christmas Day and a fortnight later all foreigners were ordered to leave. The new regulations, however, were enforced in typical fashion; for three months more ships were admitted, after tedious delays, if their agents paid the Intendant a "fee," which increased as time went on from four-and-a-half to six per cent of the value of the cargo. This arrangement was terminated at length on March 10, 1802, but only after threats were made by local merchants to report to Spain this violation of the general closing order which had arrived in the meantime. These same merchants anticipated a harvest of high prices. Though the order expelling foreigners was not enforced, the "agent"-designate, Robert Young, who was not to be called a consul out of deference to Spanish dislike of this name, may have taken it seriously. At any rate, he did not repair to his post before Morton left in July, 1802, and the departing agent appointed as acting consul Vincent Gray, a Virginian, who had become established in business during the last two or three years. Morton obtained for him the Captain-General's courtesy without recognition and Gray took over the duties, which he considered neither desirable nor profitable. He was not immediately overworked, for the new policy cut trade down ninety per cent.

The interlude did not last long. In the first place, Havana immediately suffered a shortage. Spain had returned to monopolies as usual and Count Jaruco once more had flour; but these favorites had not been enterprising enough. Havana needed at least 7000 barrels of flour a month and 10,-000 feet of lumber, so United States vessels were occasionally and grudgingly admitted. Then Great Britain and France resumed hostilities in May, 1803, and though Spain was not immediately involved, the advent of privateers in West Indian waters made Spanish shipping unsafe. The Cuban ports therefore became more hospitable to United States vessels. Gray soon had to report the old story that French privateers were capturing United States shipping with connivance of Spanish port officials. Blakely supplied a list of thirty-seven United States vessels brought into Santiago as French prizes, and destitute sailors came to the consuls in flocks for aid. Finally, on December 12, 1804, Spain entered the war itself and as usual was forced to open its colonial ports. In February, 1805, Havana was once again in need of provisions and United States ships had free access to its wharves.

This next interval of trade took on a new significance because of the *haute politique* and the imperialism of the Jefferson régime. In the interim, the United States had purchased Louisiana and was seeking to acquire Florida. Spain was angry and fearful, and though compelled to admit the United States flag to its Cuban ports, was more than ever suspicious of the United States and nervous as to the republic's possible designs upon Cuba. Now that the United States possessed the port of New Orleans, trade with Cuba was even more desirable than before and more convenient. Cuba was being drawn too close to the United States and Cuban officials were more than ever disposed to be friendly to France as a protective device. Trade, while it flourished, was in a more precarious situation and the attendant dangers greater.

## IV

The altered conditions influenced Jefferson to pursue a new policy. Under the Federalists, especially when Pickering was in office, there had been much interest in the possibilities of trade promotion, but when Jefferson came into power his policies were different. Foreign commerce was not to his mind so much a national interest as it was a national weapon. He sought, therefore, not to promote it—he did not believe in government interference to aid private interests —but to use it as an adjunct to his diplomacy.

From Jefferson's vivid interest were to stem four notable American policies: the acquisition of Florida, the protection of Cuba, the Monroe Doctrine, and Pan-Americanism. President Jefferson at first had taken no interest in Cuba, but the acquisition of Louisiana and his hopes regarding Florida needed but little time to suggest the possibility of acquiring Cuba and even Mexico. When war broke out, therefore, he

decided to send a regularly appointed agent to Cuba to relieve Gray, not so much, as we may suspect, to promote
trade as to watch events. The Captain-General of Cuba had
jurisdiction over Florida and any movement of troops made
in that direction or toward Louisiana would start from Havana. Henry Hill, Jr., of Connecticut, was appointed consul
and instructed not only in the usual form to safeguard
United States commerce and seamen, but also specifically
to report any unusual military or naval activity which might
be preparing for Florida or Louisiana. Besides commission-
ing Hill, Secretary Madison protested to the Captain-General against friendly connivance with the French and instructed the minister at Madrid to do the same. Under the
circumstances these could only be impotent gestures.

The new consul was not like Morton or Gray; he was a
forthright man who spoke his mind and who was jealous
of his dignity and bold in attack. He was to have full charge
of affairs on the island, was to supersede both Gray and
Blakely, and was authorized to appoint vice-consuls in other
Cuban ports. He had forms and stationery printed, clearly
indicating that Henry Hill, Jr., was United States consul;
there was to be no pussyfooting or hiding his rank where
he was concerned. Necessarily, his career was short and
turbulent. When he arrived in June, 1805, he found that
Gray had recently been arrested on a charge of connivance in
smuggling and his papers confiscated. As usual, the Captain-
General refused to recognize the new consul. Nevertheless,
Hill attempted to act; French privateers were altogether too
plentiful. He was no man for halfway measures: "Impotence
in a public officer ever attracts contempt and derision," he
once wrote. He made a thorough investigation of the Spanish
customs system and sent the State Department an elaborate
report which is his monument. When he found abuses he

protested vigorously. Such unwonted lack of finesse wounded the Captain-General, and when Hill's communications continued to increase in pugnacity, he was ordered —but in Spanish fashion—to leave. For after the order had been given nothing further was done and Hill's inquiries of the Captain-General's secretary assured him that he could continue to act. At the same time, at Santiago, Blakely was arrested for functioning as a United States agent and he forthwith fled the island. He was not much loss, as he had been dilatory in aiding seamen and perhaps not above smuggling; nevertheless, the manner of his exit was trying to United States pride. Discouraged by his lack of success, Hill took a prolonged leave of absence early in 1806 and left his duties to his secretary, John L. Ramage.

Jefferson and Madison perceived that Hill's methods were too forthright, and accordingly decided to send him to Jamaica. Heavy spoliations during the summer by privateers still demanded action and Jefferson's fertile brain was at work over new ideas; Miranda had talked to him of independence for the Spanish colonies and aid to the United States in case the latter went to war with Spain. The United States might acquire Mexico as well as Florida and Cuba, and put an end to much of the privateering menace. At any rate, more discreet agents, Maurice Rogers and Jacob Clement of Pennsylvania, were sent to Santiago and Puerto Rico, and in January, 1807, James Anderson of South Carolina was transferred from Cette in the south of France to Havana. Though the latter was not to be called consul, as that title caused too much trouble, but simply an agent for seamen and commerce, he was instructed to carry on the consular duties and, like Hill, was to keep watch.

Anderson proved to be the exact antithesis of Hill, for he was cautious to the degree of being fearful. He had, indeed, no pleasant task in extricating himself from the precarious position in which the "inconsiderate conduct of Mr. Hill" had placed him. He feared to report any abuses lest he might be denounced and thrown into prison. He was not even going to keep any records for, thought he, "I conceive it unnecessary and impolitic to run any risque whatever in being too particular." Besides, he feared lest he be assassinated. Nevertheless, there were compensations; like his predecessors he went into business and, including his official fees, expected to gross $10,000 a year, though his expenses were so great that he anticipated a net profit of but $3000, no small income in 1807. His realizations exceeded his prospects; nevertheless, he lamented that he would rather make one half as much in a pleasanter country, and he continued to be "poisoned with the thoughts of being stabbed should I become an object worthy the attention of assassins." Naturally, such an agent did not command much respect and Anderson complained that the ship captains "don't pay much attention to the consul"; for they often waited days before reporting with their registers. Duties, too, were raised to thirty-eight per cent on imports and twelve-and-a-half per cent on exports, and were so high that the consul was sure Americans were losing money on their trade. Yet on they came in spite of the yellow fever that raged during the summer of 1807.

The days of prosperous trading, alas, were numbered. The United States embargo of December, 1807, did less than might be supposed to limit trade because it was quite generally violated; the colonists again needed badly a market for their sugar. Anderson reported in February, 1808, that 104 United States vessels had arrived since the first of the year. The great blow came rather when Napoleon deposed the Spanish monarch in favor of Joseph Bonaparte. This error caused the remnant of the Spanish legitimate government to welcome the aid of Great Britain. In the colonies, especially in Cuba, there was an instant reaction against the French and a sudden cordiality to the British. Great Britain now had the freedom of Cuban ports and Spanish commerce had the protection of the British fleet. The monopoly which the United States had enjoyed was shattered and the United States merchants must compete with British and Spanish traders.

## V

Jefferson was both plagued and stimulated by the new developments. This sudden friendship of Spain for Great Britain was not to his liking, for the latter might take advantage of Spain's weakness and annex some of its American empire. On the other hand, France seemed about to control all of it. The United States was in danger and Jefferson's hopes of acquiring Florida, Cuba, and Mexico flared up, egged on occasionally by Napoleon's duplicity. Though Jefferson gave no open encouragement to a Cuban delegation which visited him to suggest the annexation of their island by the United States to save it from Napoleon, he considered the question in cabinet. France and Great Britain must not take territory in the Western Hemisphere.

When Madison came to the White House on March 4, 1809, he did not share Jefferson's enthusiasm for acquiring Cuba but he did carry out Jefferson's defensive policy. Anderson was sent back to Cuba to arrange for an interview between the president's personal messenger and the Captain-General. This agent, none other than the intriguing General James Wilkinson, carried the Jefferson message in terms anticipating the Monroe Doctrine. The Spanish-

American colonies might remain loyal to Spain or free themselves, but they must not fall under the sway of Britain or
France. Better let there be freedom from Spain and an independent, republican America. This gesture only frightened
the Spanish officials and increased their long-standing fears
of American designs on Florida and Cuba.

As the Captain-General and the Intendent of Cuba were
no longer dependent upon United States trade they were in
a position to vent their dislike of Americans upon those who
came to their ports. Spain's own ships were given advantages in duties which made competition with them difficult;
Great Britain's trade in these areas increased; United States
vessels were seized by the Spanish on the ground that they
were violating the embargo. The flush days for the United
States were over. By midsummer of 1809 Anderson and
Gray, who still acted as consuls occasionally, were compelled
to close the consulate and Anderson came back to the United
States. Rogers remained in Santiago until his death in 1811
but he ceased reporting after the spring of 1809 and there is
no evidence that Clement at Puerto Rico ever functioned.
Trade dropped off fifty per cent. No further attempt at re-
establishing United States agents was to be made until conditions were changed by revolution.

During this thirty years of experience a small company
of agents had led the way. Traders had tasted the profits of
Hispanic-American trade. A large number of individuals
had gained first-hand experience regarding Hispanic-American conditions. Both the mercantile class and the State
Department had learned how difficult, if not well-nigh impossible, it was to have satisfactory relationships, official
or commercial, with colonies ruled so arbitrarily and capri-
ciously, and how much must depend upon the caliber of
their agents. The knowledge thus acquired was cherished, for

these experiments in trade and diplomacy had stimulated ideas of great future significance, such as the acquisition of Florida, special interest in Cuba, the Monroe Doctrine, and Pan-Americanism.

# 3. Around the Horn

THE adventurous agents of the United States were not content to limit the bounds of their interest in the Spanish Empire to the shores of the Caribbean. Far to the southward, washed by two oceans, was South America, the great continental domain of Spain. Few Yankees had sought its tight-locked ports but when the repercussions of the French Revolution began to spring the bolts, the royal order of 1797 spelled opportunity in South America as well as in the West Indies. One of the first to take advantage of this new opportunity was a young Connecticut sea captain who was to have much to do with extending his country's interest and its knowledge of the far places of the earth.

The career of this sea captain, William Shaler, is typical of the adventurous life lived by so many of the advance agents of the new republic. These men were not only adventurers in the physical sense, dominated by desires for sight of new shores, acquaintance with strange people and possession of new wealth. They were intellectual adventurers who sought to discover new knowledge and particularly to spread the fame of American ideas and the influence of American free institutions. Likewise, they were propagandists striving to carry afar the gospel of American enlightenment. They were apostles of rational liberty.

Shaler was born in Bridgeport, Connecticut, on the eve of the American Revolution. He owed his being and his talents to his Connecticut ancestors, many of whom were

50

seafarers. Thomas Shaler had come from Stratford on Avon via Jamaica and appeared in Connecticut in 1662 as one of the original settlers at Haddam. His son and grandson were residents of Middletown. This pleasant town though far up the Connecticut River had a harbor with a ten-foot draft at flood tide and, in those days of small things, ocean-going craft could make it a port. As the fertile fields of the vicinage produced surplus crops, a thriving trade was developed with the West Indies from this bustling port.

William Shaler's father, Timothy, married Sibbel Warner of a like seafaring family in 1769 and they decided to buy land and establish a home right at the mouth of the Connecticut. They raised their rooftree in present-day Bridgeport, at that time described as Newfield, in the parish of Stratfield in the town of Stratford. Newfield was a relatively new settlement and here on a stretch of shore where the Pequannock River met Long Island Sound, Timothy and Sibbel Shaler established their home near the foot of Golden Hill. Here William was born in 1773.

Captain Timothy Shaler was destined to take part in the American Revolution during the youth of his oldest son. Although many of his family were Tories, he became a Patriot and turned his merchantman into a privateer. His sloop, the *Lyon*, was so commissioned and adventurously bore her crew of eighty men and her armament of ten guns. His shore home was exposed to Tory raids and British attack, and so for safety Captain Shaler moved his family to a less exposed community during the course of the conflict. When William was eight his mother died and five years later, in 1786, his father was stricken with apoplexy and William, his two younger brothers, and a sister were orphans. The executor of their father's estate mismanaged and dissipated it, and at the age of fourteen the youth became responsible for the family livelihood.

He was apprenticed in the countinghouse of Nathaniel G. Ingraham of the New York trading firm of Ingraham, Phoenix and Nixsen, where he learned the business and also obtained "considerable proficiency in the Study of History and miscellaneous literature." At the conclusion of his apprenticeship he had made such progress that he was designated as supercargo on a succession of trading voyages and was entrusted with the responsibility of handling a good deal of money. His first ventures were carrying goods from the French West Indies to France, through the perils of the privateering which flourished after the outbreak of the war in 1793. He and his younger brother, Nathaniel, who became a ship captain in these exciting years, had many adventurous encounters with British naval vessels and learned to discount danger heavily.

Contact with France and wariness of the British roused his sympathy for the French cause and he fell under the spell of the French revolutionary enthusiasm. Thus the cause of liberty called him as it had his father during the days of his first remembrance. More important, he became dissatisfied with his lack of education. As his only biographer described it, "The early impressions made on his mind by the precepts of his excellent mother, seemed now to become more vivid, and he began to feel a deep sense of his want of mental cultivation, which induced him to see about teaching himself." He learned the French language, studied French history, and read French philosophical works "with the same enthusiasm in which many of them were written." He was reported as having a rare talent for acquiring languages and as speaking "with fluency, most of those of Europe," especially French.

His home port in France was Bordeaux where he dealt principally with John Bernard and where he was likely to hear much of trading opportunities in the remote regions of Asia and Africa. He was always on the lookout for fields for new ventures and the European conflict was providing them in great number. The news that the Spanish had thrown open their American ports under the order of November 18, 1797, traveled slowly, but eventually it came to Shaler and Bernard and they saw new opportunities. They decided to send a cargo to a most distant spot, to the Spanish ports on the La Plata in South America. Few traders had ever gone there and now that the British had cut Spain off from her colonies, there should be a yawning market. So they loaded the ship *Friends* with a miscellaneous cargo of French wines, silk stockings, English "brittania ware," cambric, paper, and other items. James Christie was hired as captain to sail the ship with Shaler as supercargo under contract of January 11, 1799.

Thus manned and freighted, the *Friends* set sail from Bordeaux and made the long voyage to the La Plata, arriving at Montevideo on May 20, 1799. Here they found themselves among the very first to reach the ports opened to a new freedom. Only three or four had preceded them when they began their trade. There were two ports of significance on the La Plata, where they centered their efforts. The first was Montevideo, a new town perched on a gentle elevation at the end of a small peninsula under the shadow of the mountain from which it derived its name. It owed its existence to its fine harbor, and its Spanish founders had built it according to the stock plan which they used wherever possible. Its unpaved streets with their one-story buildings stretched out from the public square around which stood the cathedral, the *cabildo,* and the prison. The town was either a cloud of dust or a sea of mud. Wood was lacking, as the rolling country of the region had few trees, consequently even the floors of the houses had to be made of bricks. Water likewise was scarce and had to be carried from springs two miles from the port. Trade was the center of attention. Here Shaler engaged the services of the necessary agent, Don B. de Sorias, for foreigners themselves could not trade. Through him they arranged for dealings with Buenos Aires.

This second city was two hundred miles up the estuary on the opposite shore at a point where the river was thirty-one miles wide. The river was dangerous and difficult of navigation, and most vessels had to anchor some four miles from the city and discharge their cargoes to smaller craft. The alternative was to anchor off the port of Ensenada and transport the goods thirty-two miles overland. The city itself numbered 40,000 inhabitants and was laid out in the prevailing Spanish colonial mode. Its streets were paved and its houses were larger, generally of two stories. It had many churches, ministered to by 1100 priests, and the bells clanged all day long. The region itself had prevailing fogs in these summer months which were their winter, and occasionally the community was torn by great hurricanes, the Pamperas, blowing up from the Pampas.

Shaler plied between these ports all summer. Try as he might he could not sell all of his cargo of wines, although he disposed of all the rest of the goods and some of the liquor for $34,734.25, most of it at Montevideo. He reinvested part of the proceeds in tallow, wheat and flour, and finally in September he left the Plata estuary.

Shaler is next discovered within three months at Mauritius, on the Isle of France, a victim of privateers. This was the period of French hostility to the United States which had precipitated the "Quasi-War" with that power, and

French privateers were busy with American commerce. The Isle of France, in the Indian Ocean some distance from the east coast of Africa, was the headquarters of an extensive privateering fleet. On its return voyage to France, the *Friends* had been captured and taken into Port Louis, or Port Northwest as it was then called. Here the boat was sold as a prize, and Shaler was forced to settle down to await some means of getting away from this distant island.

Shaler lived with the American Consul and found plenty of time to study his interesting surroundings. Save the port, the island was a community of planters specializing in cotton, coffee, and indigo. The neighboring island of Bourbon, or Reunion, was even richer in plantation produce but as it had no safe port, this wealth was shipped over to the Isle of France and there exported from Port Louis. This town where Shaler must perforce wait was a small place of some 15,000 residents of whom two-thirds were slaves. The houses were of wood, one or two stories high, low because high winds made greater height dangerous. The streets were unpaved, lined with mimosa trees which in season had beautiful blossoms. The climate was mild, in fact many Negroes went practically naked. The altitude of the town and of the island inhabitants in general was frankly speculative. Planters came to get rich, sell out, and go back to France. The merchants were living in expectation of prizes of war.

Shaler found other Americans who had sought the consulate, like himself, and in May, 1800, he was joined by another sea rover with whom the rest of his life was to be entwined. Richard J. Cleveland had come from India in a small ship expecting to buy a prize vessel cheap. However, there were none available at a sufficiently low price, so he, like Shaler, had to settle down at the consular residence. In November the privateer *Confiance* brought in an East India

Company ship which was sold to a Dane who renamed her the *Cronberg*. Then the Dane could find no one willing to ship a cargo because French property would probably be seized by the British. So at length the Dane came to Shaler and Cleveland and suggested that they buy coffee and other island products and freight them very reasonably to Copenhagen. They agreed and set to work to make up a cargo.

There were some delays and it was not until March 21, 1801, fifteen months after Shaler had landed, that they were ready to start. They had a safe passage around the Cape of Good Hope and arrived off the coast of Denmark in eighty days, without meeting the British. However, they were then surprised with news that England and Denmark were at war and that Copenhagen, their destination, was the center of conflict. Happily, hostilities were almost over, and they soon were able to dispose of their cargo as planned and look to another venture which they had discussed upon their long voyage.

These adventurous mariners had a new and relatively unknown field as the object of their daring. Shaler had ventured in the Spanish-American empire as it faced the Atlantic, but that empire had a great Pacific shore which had theoretically always been closed to ships flying other flags than the Spanish. In fact, Spain had attempted to call the Pacific a closed sea. American whalers, however, were in the habit of seeking their livelihood in this vast ocean and were not above attempting to trade at Valparaiso, Callao, and other west-coast ports. As early as Washington's administration the State Department protested the Spanish custom of warning United States ships to stay out of the Pacific, and Timothy Pickering, then Secretary, declared that the right of navigating that, or any other sea, was too important to be renounced. Spain refused to concede his contention but about this time it became possible for whalers to get permits from John Stoughton, Spanish consul at Boston, in the fashion of Jaudenes and Viar. The smuggling still continued.

Now Shaler and Cleveland thought the time ripe for more legitimate traffic because of the royal order of 1797, still in effect despite its revocation by the Spanish government. The west-coast ports would be fine sources of profits because the war had so long cut them off from Spain that their stocks would be sure to be low. Shaler and Cleveland might dispose of a cargo here, then sail northward to the Oregon shores, pick up a load of furs and sail to China. A third cargo might be gathered at Canton and then sail ho! for home with a fortune large enough to permit these ancient mariners, aged thirty, to retire in opulence.

There was more to their venture than trade. They had a mission as well, a mission to scatter a few seeds of liberty. Shaler was planning to take books for study. He desired to learn the Spanish language and write down his impressions of the strange lands he was to visit. In his baggage were copies of the Declaration of Independence in Spanish and samples of the American constitutions, state and federal. The wealth they sought would be used to promote educational and scientific objectives, for each of these young mariners had the desire to live eventually in the world of letters. The path they had chosen proved difficult.

Copenhagen presented no opportunity to buy a ship such as they wanted so they decided to proceed to Hamburg where there was an extensive American trade, in the hope of finding what they needed. Their quest was successful and they purchased a stanch vessel of one hundred and seventy-five tons, the *Lelia Byrd* of Portsmouth, Virginia. This purchase concluded, Shaler went back to Bordeaux to settle his accounts with John Bernard. In spite of the misfortunes of his voyage he had some forty thousand francs from which he paid his accounts, left the balance with Bernard at interest and made him executor of his will in which he provided particularly for his sister Abigail.

The *Lelia Byrd* was now ready but she needed a captain and as Shaler and Cleveland were equally interested and neither wanted the responsibility, they drew lots and Shaler had to assume the command. This duumvirate, however, was to be augmented by the addition of a third companion. At Hamburg they met a young Pole, Count de Rouissillon, former aid to Kosciusko. He was a cultured young man of twenty-eight who loved liberty and had suffered banishment for her sake. He was eager to see the world and his pleasant manners were sure to make him good company. The captains had suffered the tedium of long voyages and they welcomed a congenial spirit. Nor were they disappointed. He brought a library of Russian, Polish, and German books which he continually studied and which they all enjoyed discussing. As Cleveland later recorded, he was a man of untiring industry who seemed to grudge a moment that passed without adding something to his knowledge. Even when walking on the deck he would practice on his flute.

The voyage of these companions did not start auspiciously. Just as they were ready, peace broke out in Europe and raised grave doubts as to whether there might be any entrance into Spanish-American ports. Yet, they did not allow themselves to be deterred. Then when they set sail from Cuxhaven, November 8, 1801, they were beset by a great storm which nearly ended their career. Safely through this peril, they found a pleasant recess at the Canaries and their voyage across the Atlantic was serene. On New Year's Day, they came within sight of the picturesque harbor of

Rio de Janeiro, but the Portuguese inhospitably gave them leave to remain only a few days, to replenish their supplies and try to sell some of their goods to Spanish traders from the La Plata ports then in the harbor. They enjoyed the beauties of the town and its environs for this limited time but were disappointed in their efforts to trade. Eight days after their arrival, they must perforce depart upon the always formidable voyage around the Horn. Their voyage had its share of danger and tragedy, for in the mighty storms they encountered, they lost one of the crew overboard. But at length, forty-five days out from Rio, they arrived at Valparaiso, February 24, 1802.

This port they found located on a semicircular bay surrounded by steep slopes rising abruptly from the water's edge. The houses clung to the sides of these hills, and the principal street climbed steeply from the sea, lined with houses and shops. Various other streets had been built up ravines, where houses rose one above the other so that the roofs were often overlooked by the windows of the ground-floor rooms of the next neighbors. At night the lights of these dwellings twinkled in scattered profusion on the hillsides. Quite a portion of the population lived in the suburbs hidden in a sort of recess in the hills, on a sandy plain. In the center of the metropolis was one of the fortifications which also served as a dwelling for the governor. The town had a wall fifteen feet high flanked by other fortifications to the north and south.

The entrance of the mariners into this harbor was ominous of what was to come. There they saw four American vessels riding at anchor. Their own ship was boarded immediately by a naval officer who forbade the casting of their anchor until the captain had waited on the acting governor to seek permission. Mr. Shaler, therefore, proceeded to land.

The local governor was away and his *locum tenens*, García Carrasco, was a somewhat large edition of pompous vanity who informed Shaler that only the Captain-General Muñoz Guzmán could grant permission to stay even long enough to buy necessary provisions. So Shaler must hire an "express," or messenger to carry a petition to the inland capital, and in the meantime there was nothing to do but wait. Shaler, therefore, returned to the ship anticipating no particular difficulty, for purchase of provisions was duly provided by the Spanish treaty. But what were so many American ships doing there? In due time he discovered that they were being detained, charged with smuggling and supplying British privateers while ostensibly operating as whalers and sealers. Their plight made the new arrivals indignant and gave them another object, that of aiding their distressed brethren and maintaining American rights.

Three days later the messenger returned from the capital with a command to leave within twenty-four hours. Wrote the Captain-General, after so favorable a passage the visitors could not need provisions and, besides, the bills on Paris which they wished to use for purchasing were not receivable in this province. The fact was that Spain had received reports of this voyage from Hamburg and had warned the Captain-General to watch this ship. Shaler, nothing daunted, went back to the local governor and dilated so on the inhumanity of driving the vessel out to sea unprovisioned that the functionary permitted them to wait until another request might be considered in which the exigencies of the occasion might be more vividly set forth. The acting governor professed to be sympathetic and promised to urge the necessity. But only a second order to leave resulted.

Shaler was suspicious now and determined to try out his

newly acquired Spanish. So he wrote a letter himself to the Captain-General, explaining that he presumed that "his Excellency's intentions" had been misconceived by the local governor, so he had ventured to disobey the order and remain in port until the reception of his Excellency's own reply. Shaler's Spanish was sufficiently eloquent to gain immediate permission to stay, to buy what was needed, and further, although it had not been requested, to sell such part of the cargo as might be necessary to pay for what was bought. Then, however, the mariners must depart and make no further landing along the coast on pain of seizure as smugglers.

The indignation of the three republican enthusiasts at this latter implication did not prevent them from taking full advantage of the more liberal permission. They sold what they could and at length prepared to leave after more than four weeks of sojourn in this Valparaiso, vale of paradise, so called. Then adventure overtook them once more.

Captain Rowan of the *Hazard*, one of the vessels under detention, had several hundred muskets which he had purchased in Holland and which he intended to use in trading on the northwest coast. The acting governor of Valparaiso now took it into his rather inconsequential head to demand these guns. Rowan refused, whereupon the governor took his garrison of some thirty men in a launch to enforce his demands. The American was not taken by surprise, for he had armed sailors awaiting the expedition. Nonplused at this show of resistance, the governor returned to land in a rage. He ordered all Americans on shore to be seized and thrown into prison. As Shaler, Cleveland, and Rouissillon were all ashore they fell victims to his violence and were hustled to the castle. Meanwhile, the governor ordered a Spanish armed vessel to point its guns at the *Hazard* and demand the ship's surrender. In reply Rowan nailed his colors to the mast.

Such defiance threw the foolish governor into further tantrums and he sent off to Santiago for permission to take more violent measures. Not until next morning did he bethink himself of the prisoners. Shaler and his companions for their part had been having a most uncomfortable time in the castle. There were no beds, there was nothing to eat, and there were fleas—swarms of them. They passed part of the night writing a letter to the governor asking for food and better equipment. He in his turn, in dudgeon, sent the letter back unopened. By noon, however, he awakened to the embarrassment of holding prisoners who were under no accusation. He thereupon sent a guard to tell them they could go. But not so fast! During the flea-ridden night there had hatched an idea. There might be hope of a trip to Santiago yet, and further trade if they could once see the Captain-General, for they had learned subterraneously that if they did get to Santiago they might arrange the sale of the cargo to be delivered at sea at a very good price. The chance was worth fighting for. They would demand an apology, an investigation, and a chance to testify on behalf of Rowan. Consequently Shaler, as captain of the ship, refused to leave the prison. His friends however went out to buy him a bed and something to eat.

The governor rushed to the prison to beg Shaler to go, but Shaler demanded a written apology which was refused. Then he demanded permission to send a messenger to the Captain-General; this message met the same fate with even greater display of temper. The functionary then went out on the streets, met Cleveland and ordered him to take the ship to sea immediately. Cleveland refused to go without the captain and affairs were at an impasse.

Next day, to the governor's chagrin, the Captain-General sent a message which was fair and conciliatory and caused Rowan to surrender the guns. All might then have been fair sailing but for the governor's pride. He had been flouted, he thought, and his small mind banished all its slight contents except the idea of revenge. On a trumped-up charge he got two hundred local thugs and Spanish sailors to storm and plunder the *Hazard* when none were on guard. This was done with great gusto; two American sailors were wounded and Rowan escaped with his life only by a miracle.

Here was another opportunity to make demands for justice; and Cleveland went immediately to the governor. There was a pretty scene which ended by the Spaniard threatening similar treatment for the *Lelia Byrd*. But the American faced him so boldly that the governor yielded to the demand for permission and off went the express with a letter in Shaler's hand, which was improving by use. The letter sent, Shaler a few days later bade good-by to the greater number of the fleas and returned to the *Lelia Byrd*.

The correspondence that resulted was lengthy, and while it ran its slow course, Shaler and his companions took advantage of their notoriety to talk with some of the leading creoles. Naturally, they spoke of rights, justice, liberty, and the profits of free trade. As they got better acquainted they learned how discontented many were with the restrictions and tyrannies of Spain, and their new acquaintances showed keen interest in the ideas of rational liberty which the strangers described with such enthusiasm. Out came the Spanish translations of the Declaration of Independence and the other pamphlets, and far into the night the discussion waxed eloquent. Almost, the star of liberty seemed gleaming in the Chilean heavens.

The Captain-General was not so captivated by their elo-
quence. After an extensive exchange of letters in which
Shaler argued vigorously that the Spanish could not expect
to rule the Pacific Ocean and bar out the ships of the non-
Spanish world, the Captain-General concluded the whole
matter by the incontestable assertion that at least they
could control their own harbors. Therefore as Shaler and
his friends could find no further pretext for remaining, on
April 19th, nearly two months after their arrival, they prepared to depart. But not yet. They were shipping a number
of the crews of the stranded vessels to carry them to Mas-a-
Fuera where they might expect to find other whalers and
new berths. The increase of the human complement led the
governor to fear they were getting ready to attack a Spanish
vessel about to sail to Lima, so he detained the *Byrd* yet
two more days. Just as the ship was to sail on April 23rd,
another of the now regularly occurring surprises hove to.

The captain of two privateers frequenting the port sent
a lieutenant on board the *Byrd* with a request that Shaler
bring him the ship's papers. How a privateer could have any
authority, Shaler could not see, and he replied that after
breakfast he would go to the governor. However, as both
the ships now began to get ready for action and as all re-
membered how the *Hazard* had been treated, Shaler thought
better of it and went on board the privateer. There he was
confronted with a charge made by an Irish sailor who had
deserted from the *Byrd,* that Shaler and Cleveland were
hiding specie. The captain, acting for the governor then, put
Shaler's seamen in irons on the privateer and searched the
*Byrd.* In the exact place the deserter described, kegs were
found, but instead of specie they contained quicksilver
which was not contraband. Finding no specie the captain

then assured Shaler that his men would be returned and his ship be speeded away in the morning. Another false hope; instead, the privateer sent his own men on board and instead of speeding the ship they confiscated ten kegs of the quicksilver, quite carelessly breaking open two and losing most of the contents.

So the tragic farce had to begin all over again. Another demand was sent to Santiago both for redress and for permission to come to Santiago. Several days later came the usual refusal of permission to travel inland and an assurance that all could be settled speedily by the simple process of filling out a questionnaire:

Why was the quicksilver hidden?

To whom did it belong?

What port was it destined for?

So Shaler must go before the governor and in the presence of a notary take solemn oath that:

The silver was not hidden.

That it belonged to the owners of the cargo.

That its destination was round the world.

To the truth of these statements Shaler made oath on a volume of Shakespeare.

Now the comedy of errors was about played out. On May 1st, the real governor of Valparaiso returned from his extended sojourn in Santiago and his scatterbrained *locum tenens* had no further opportunity to exercise his unusually peculiar talents. On Monday Shaler called on the real governor. Tuesday the quicksilver was returned. Wednesday Shaler and Cleveland refused to enter a trap when a customhouse officer offered to buy the silver clandestinely and Thursday, May 6th, the *Lelia Byrd* set sail, her masters somewhat poorer in purse but much richer in practical knowledge of the Spanish mind. Yet it had not been in vain; they had preached the gospel of liberty and had gained knowledge of great value; both achievements were to bear fruit in later time.

# 4. Hither and Yon Across the Pacific

THE quixotic turn of events of the last months showed conclusively that no further trading operations could be undertaken by Shaler in South America, for the Captain-General at Santiago had warned the Viceroy in Lima. So whither? The western coast of Mexico or New Spain seemed the only alternative and another long course was charted. More watery weeks were marked off, broken only by a stop at the Galápagos Islands; in fact they sailed for two months without sighting a sail. At length, July 11th, they arrived at San Blas. What a contrast when compared with Valparaiso!

The town itself was on a hill overlooking a bay which offered a convenient harbor except for the summer months when the prevailing southeast winds and thunder squalls made it dangerous for vessels, and the unhealthful climate menaced human welfare. The town presented a pleasant appearance when first approached, but upon landing the adventurers found its streets dirty and the houses of no particular quality. There was little commerce; the principal importance of the place and the reason for its five thousand inhabitants was the royal arsenal with seven hundred employees. As this was the season of the summer exodus to the more salubrious hinterland, only subordinates were in the town, but their cordial welcome indicated a different spirit. And the fact that the Intendant came from Tipec,

67

the summer capital, to greet them was further evidence of good will.

With this functionary they easily entered into business arrangements, especially as they had some tin which was much in demand. However, before any transactions could be completed the approval of the Governor must be had, and he was in Tipec. As Rouissillon was anxious to visit Mexico City, he volunteered to go to Tipec with the Intendant, not only to complete the business arrangements, but to gain permission to go to the capital. Their pleasant introduction, however, was the end of their good fortune.

Once again they ran afoul of the peculiarities of the Spanish system of colonial government. The Governor and the Intendant were of equal rank and authority, and independent of each other in most of their functions. In this case the Governor was extremely jealous and "difficult," therefore he resented the Intendant's negotiations with the newcomers and refused all sanction. This chagrined the Intendant. Both aired their grievances, and soon the sleepy little town of Tipec was an armed camp, figuratively speaking. Each official had his partisans and at least one army officer went to jail for his support of the Intendant. The net result was a peremptory order from the governor for the boat to leave. Rouissillon, however, was to proceed to Mexico City to see if he could gain the needed trading permit. The three partners had anticipated some such possibility and had prepared for it. Shaler and Cleveland would obey the order and sail away, but only about sixty miles, where they would tarry at the Tres Marías Islands until sufficient time had elapsed for Rouissillon to have accomplished his errand. They would return to San Blas whenever an Indian messenger might bring word from him.

At first they enjoyed the freedom of life on and off shore

at Tres Marías; they fished, they explored the islands, they overhauled the boat, but at length it got monotonous, and as no word came their anxiety increased. Finally, Shaler and Cleveland decided to risk a return, if only to gain tidings of their comrade. Ten weeks after their departure, therefore, they returned, taking care to approach San Blas with great caution. To their great relief, a canoe full of Indians appeared and handed up the long-awaited letter from their absent comrade. He had received permission to go to Mexico with some assurance of success and the Viceroy had so rebuked the Governor that the reprimand had destroyed the balance of his feeble health and he had died. Such a fortunate turn of events left but one problem, namely, how to await the outcome of Rouissillon's trip. If they tarried at San Blas they would have to tolerate a Spanish guard on the ship. Rather than put up with that they decided to go back to the Tres Marías. After a repetition of their former experiences in this pleasant spot, though for a much shorter interval, they returned for a second time to San Blas.

The reception of the local authorities was more cordial than ever, but unfortunately a letter was awaiting them from Rouissillon. This time the news was not good. To be sure he had arrived safely enough and had been received. Also after some discreet corruption he had obtained a permission to sell $10,000 worth of the cargo. Further than that he could report no progress. Only by surrendering all the profits to interested officialdom could he gain permission to sell the entire cargo. He immediately followed his letter and on December 10th returned. The $10,000 sale permitted was so small in quantity that few merchants would take the trouble to travel far to participate and there were not many local men. Little business could be done on that basis. However, a cargo of otter skins had arrived from

California and a plan was worked out to purchase this cargo which Shaler and Cleveland should take north for further venturing, while Rouissillon was to keep $3000 worth of the manufactured goods and sell them, it was hoped, for three times that sum, joining his companions later in the United States to give an account. They, however, never heard from him again. Somehow, somewhere in Mexico he died that same year and they could gain no trace of their property in his charge.

At the last moment they were once again in danger of losing everything because a disgruntled mate had told the local authorities of their difficulties at Valparaiso and, had the commandant of the guard not been interested in the otter-skin trade, they might have been imprisoned. As it was, they were in fear until the last moment and risked a final controversy with the authorities to gain sufficient delay to get the precious skins aboard. These last few days were made tense by persistent rumors that a custom's guard was on its way to search the *Lelia Byrd,* but at length by a ruse they departed a day early and thus eluded whatever danger there may have been. At length, January 25, 1803, they were once more out of Spanish jurisdiction. Here, too, Shaler had had close contact with the Spaniards. Here he had spread propaganda. He had found the creoles disaffected, fearful of the Indians, and ready to listen to the plausibilities of rational liberty. Likewise, the usual administrative ineffectiveness and capriciousness had added to his stock of information regarding the far places of the earth and the vagaries of human conduct.

Once again the cordial Tres Marías welcomed the venturers. The worms had been playing havoc with the stout ship's hull, and now it must be careened and boot-topped, as the old salts say. Such a task was something of a test, with the limited facilities at hand for a crew of fifteen, and was only accomplished with difficulty. A fortnight of hard work was made more tense by a final confirmation of Shaler's suspicions regarding the mate. He was a wrong-headed young English sailor who got so unmanageable that he had to be relieved of duty. He still had his place at the officers' table, with complete freedom but no responsibility. From some remarks he had made to sailors, Shaler suspected he had trafficked with the officials at San Blas, and that he had failed to do more damage only because he hadn't started his negotiations until after the San Blas authorities had made business commitments to the Americans, which would have been uncovered if they had seized the vessel. Shaler and Cleveland now inspected his papers and found these suspicions verified; the mate had told of the difficulties with the Spanish at Valparaiso.

St. Valentine's Day, 1803, at length became the day of their departure and it was "Ho for California!" where at San Diego, they had learned, there were more otter skins. Not until St. Patrick's Day did they reach this desired haven. Here a third adventure with Hispanic-American temperament was at hand.

The harbor of San Diego provided a roadstead and anchorage about three miles from the town and here the *Lelia Byrd* dropped anchor. Next morning came a pageant of ridiculous grandeur. Comandante Don Manuel Rodriguez, resplendent in fine clothes and escorted by twelve dragoons, appeared alongside and climbed to the deck. There, in solemn state, he stood while his escort formed in double line with hats doffed and swords drawn; then and not till then did His Excellency advance to the companionway. With great ceremony he made the usual inquiries, ordered his officer to take note of the supplies required by Shaler, and with awful dignity assured the visitors that their needs would be filled next day, whereupon they must delay not a moment in leaving the port. They must not approach nearer the town but they might go ashore at this point. Five of the guards were to remain on board, and with great ceremony he took his departure.

Several days later when the supplies had been delivered the commandant once more appeared. He resisted all importunities to sell otter skin, knowing that such sale would be discovered by some of his subordinates and duly reported to Spain, and concluded by a further order to leave. But if the captain would not make a sale, there seemed others who would. Various people had rowed out to bargain, promising delivery after dark. Therefore, on the last night, the ship's boats were sent to rendezvous but one of them failed to return. At dawn the boat was discovered lying on the shore and a short distance away lay the three men of the crew bound and under guard.

Shaler now suspected that this clandestine trade was a plot on the part of the vainglorious "comandante" to find excuse for plunder. They had learned from the guard that the *Alexander* from Boston had recently been in the harbor and after the captain had bought several hundred skins the local force had boarded the vessel and plundered it. Shaler, however, was not going to be served that way. He was always ready for action. As soon as Cleveland returned from a reconnaissance, Shaler disarmed the guards on the boat and Cleveland took four men, heavily armed, ashore. These easily rescued their comrades and after submerging the arms of the shore guard in salt water returned to the ship. Shaler in the meantime had her ready for sailing and they immediately steered for the open sea. However, the wind was contrary and instead of a quick run past the fort they must proceed with such deliberation as to be within gunshot of the battery for at least an hour. It was only too plain, from observation, that the port was all a-bustle and that preparations for a bombardment were in progress: six nine-pounders were to be trained on the *Lelia Byrd*. Shaler brought all the *Lelia's* guns, six three-pounders, on the fort side and prepared for the worst. There was but one possibility of preventing a bombardment, namely, exposing the Spanish guards still on board the ship and most unhappy. But this was of no avail and for three-quarters of an hour the Spanish guns did their best. Fortunately, the marksmanship was not very effective and most of the shots which came near the mark damaged only the sails and rigging. Shaler held his fire until right abreast of the fort. Here several shots struck the hull. Now was the time for the broadside, and with what an effect! At the first, the many spectators ran pell-mell and at the second, the soldiers themselves ran. Only one remained, frantically waving his hat, as if begging that the awful firing cease. The Spanish guards to their utter amazement were put ashore and the boat sailed out of the harbor saluted by their cheers of relief. Such was the battle of San Diego, March 22, 1803.

Two days later, after sailing southward, they arrived at the Bay of St. Quintin where they met Captain Brown of the *Alexander* and compared notes. Shortly thereafter they were joined by a company of padres who came from missions, San Vincente, San Domingo, San Rosario, and San Fernando with a host of Indian retainers. These jovial friars were making a holiday of the unusual opportunity and had a well-stocked larder. They traded a few skins but spent most of their time in visiting back and forth and feasting. When they learned that the Americanos were the ones who though so ill-treated at San Diego had forborne to wreak vengeance, they were even more hospitable. When their provisions ran out they went back for more while the sailors again careened their vessel. Within two weeks the padres returned with even more provisions and the feasting began again. Finally, on May 3rd the Americans regretfully set sail for the island of Guadaloupe in search of water, sadly lacking at St. Quintin.

Guadaloupe was disappointing so Shaler steered for the coast and arrived at a point some sixty miles from the mission of San Borgia. The very next day the padre appeared on the shore with a score of servants and provisions and baggage carried by twenty-five horses and mules. Shaler invited him aboard but the motion of the ship made him sick so that next day a tent was pitched for him on shore and there his clever Indian cook spent his days in preparing a series of repasts which were pure delight to the seafaring appetites used to salt horse. Though there was no water there, Shaler and Cleveland stayed on, for so anxious was the padre to enjoy their company that he sent six miles for a sufficient supply for each day's use. All told they fell under the sway of his kindly personality. He even promised to get them horses, which they sought as a present for the King of the Hawaiian Islands. He was as good as his word. But they could not stay forever and at length departed. Once again they sailed south to the very end of the peninsula. There, at the bay of St. Joseph, they found the water they so badly needed. Here too the padres were hospitable. They purchased their last provisions, a quantity of pearls and a mare with a foal. After great difficulty this latter animal was gotten on board of the ship, and May 28th, it was heave ho! for the Sandwich Islands.

For nearly a month Shaler and Cleveland plowed their narrow furrow through the Pacific and on June 19th they

were greeted by the tall summit of "O-whyhee." The King
was supposed to be at Karakakwa Bay so they lost no time
in sailing into this harbor and firing a gun. Nothing happened, not a sign of life, but at length, after more than an
hour, two men swam out. One of them knew enough English to say that the King was at Mowee. Provisions were
needed so the vessel anchored and next day was visited by
John Young, one of the few white men on the islands. He
undertook to get the provisions and in return made urgent
request for one of the horses. The mare and her foal were
landed, the first of their kind to tread Hawaiian soil.

Sailing next to Mowee they were boarded by Isaac Davis
who with Young, some years before, had been captured
from Captain Melcalf's ship and induced to stay to help
them. Shortly thereafter, a large double canoe arrived and
a vigorous man, nearly naked, came aboard. Davis introduced him as the King. He was in a peculiarly preoccupied
state of mind, scarcely noticed anyone and hardly looked
at the horses. His visit was short and hardly polite. But in
the next few days his subjects made up for what the monarch lacked in interest. They swarmed over the ship and
were particularly intrigued by the animals. Soon, the horses
were landed and presented to the King who expressed polite
thanks with no particular enthusiasm. The crowd was elec-
trified when one of the sailors rode horseback, but the potentate was still unimpressed; in fact, he remarked that ability to carry a man faster than he could walk was not worth
the feed the animal would consume. Shaler was much disappointed and refused the small present which the King
offered in return. After a few days' search among the other
islands for yams, much needed to augment the slender supply of bread, they paid their last respects to the islands at
Atour, the westernmost of the group. At this latter island

they left a message from the King summoning that island to send an embassy to acknowledge the monarch as sovereign or suffer invasion. The European with whom they left the message said it would have no effect. Their mission completed and their supplies replenished they sailed onward to China, July 7th. They stopped at Guam and were nearly swamped in a tropical hurricane, but at length, on August 26th, they arrived in Macao Roads and by the 30th were at Canton.

Business was good there, in part at least, and the skins were disposed of for tea, and the tea almost as promptly sold to another American ship. Much of the cargo brought from Europe was still on board, so Shaler decided to take the *Lelia Byrd* back to California and the Pacific Northwest. Cleveland, on the other hand, would return home by sailing on a ship bound directly for Boston. With the help of various American crews, then at Canton, the *Lelia* was once more overhauled and gotten ready to recross the Pacific. But they were not to leave Canton without adventure. The very honorable Hong merchant who had traded "high-grade tea" for the furs had so impressed them that Shaler and Cleveland had not examined his wares. The Yankee shipper, however, with whom they traded the tea was more suspicious and his examination showed the tea to be inferior. Whereupon the Hong merchant was called to account and, rather than risk exposure, remedied the fraud though with no apology.

Shaler's return voyage across the Pacific in the leaky *Lelia* took him by Formosa and the Lew Chew Islands. Near the former he discovered an isle unrecorded on his chart which he named for Cleveland. Through a succession of hard westerly gales he steered his ship and after nearly three months he arrived off the mouth of the Columbia with a sprung foremast. He needed to put ashore for repairs but the weather was too tempestuous and he dared not cross the bar. So he sailed down the coast, enjoying its wild beauties. He was learning, as were so many to follow him, the glories of the Oregon coast. "Its mountains, rising in magnificent amphitheatres, covered with evergreen forests, with here and there a verdant plain near the shore, and a snow-capt mountain in the background, offer a view grand and sublime." After ten days off the coast he put in at Trinity Bay, now in Humboldt County, California, just north of Cape Mendocino. After making his repairs and experiencing some trying incidents with the local Indians, he finally put off for the Spanish settlements.

During the month of June he stopped at the various mission stations along the Alta California shore. Here he traded for furs and in various instances sold his wares to the padres in return for their notes. Because of the notorious affair of the battle of San Diego Shaler was unable to put into any of the fortified places like Monterrey or San Diego and had to move quietly among the missions.

He next decided on another Mexican venture so he spent the month of July sailing along the peninsula of Lower California and into the Gulf where, on August 2nd, he put in at Guaymas, in the future Mexican state of Sonora. But here the government took a hand as before and forbade any trade. As the post was poorly stocked with goods but had plenty of gold and silver, Shaler lost a fine opportunity. All he could do was attempt to repair his ship. This was none too successful as he found when he put out into the Gulf again, so he finally entered a secluded bay on the barren shore of the peninsula, unloaded everything and careened the ship on the shore in order to stop the inroads of decay and sea life on the ship's hull. This took him until October and then he tried to trade at Mazatlan with no better results. Nothing daunted, he determined to seek Central America and arrived in the Gulf of Fonseca, in present-day Honduras, at Christmastime. Here he was uninterrupted for a fortnight and was able to do some trading and make some repairs. Then the Spanish officers arrived with a large detachment of troops. These threatened to take the ship but Shaler's guns were too much for them and they soon abandoned their hostile attitude.

Shaler saw no further opportunity to profit so he set sail northward January 14, 1805, and proceeded to California once more where he traded during March and April. The old boat, however, was again badly off so he spent May on Catalina Island at a bay named Rouissillon. Work as he might, however, it was apparent that the *Lelia Byrd* would not carry him back to China, for the keel and sternpost were nearly reduced to a honeycomb. Finally on June 12th, he set forth to try and finish his trading. He traversed most of the coast once more, collected more furs and finally on July 30th set out for the Hawaiian Islands where he hoped he might find another ship. All told he had spent some seven months in California and had been much attracted by its beauty and its fertility, but particularly by its undeveloped character and the ease with which it might be taken by the United States. He was undoubtedly one of the first to catch this vision and he was not to forget it.

After another terrific storm in which the crazy ship seemed certain to founder, he arrived at O-whyhee (Hawaii) on August 19th and shortly he found a ship, the *Huron* of New Haven, which had been on a sealing voyage and was now bound for Canton. He planned to take his furs and money on this to China, but there still remained the *Lelia Byrd* with a part of her cargo still unsold. He now planned to exchange the *Byrd* for one of the small vessels of the Hawaiian king and send it back to California to dispose of the rest of the cargo under a young man, Hudson, whom they had taken on at Valparaiso. The King, Tamaihamaiha (Kamehameha), readily agreed to let him take a new schooner of forty-five tons burden which he was then building. Shaler and his carpenters aided in the finishing of the ship. While he lived on shore at Whahoo (Oahu) in a royal house with a guard of soldiers for his protection, he reveled in the climate and the bathing and entirely re-established his health "which had been reduced very low by the constant fatigue of body and mind" in these last months in the *Lelia Byrd*. He also became well acquainted with the King and learned to admire him greatly. Among other things his advice was asked upon the conquest of a rival monarch which the King was planning. The regal behavior made quite an impression upon him. As he later recorded, "Here we find an uncultivated barbarian, actuated by the same motives, and using the same specious arguments to justify his pretensions, as his brother kings of the civilized world, planning the conquest of a rival empire! Thus, from the imperial Corsican to the sable Haytian and tawny Sandwich islander, there seems to be no other difference than the means of annoyance which each possesses: their views are the same, and the result of their criminal ambition not very different: a greater or less degree of human misery."

Under the circumstances he advised the monarch against the conquest and in favor of a negotiated peace. He agreed to mediate the dispute and arranged a truce. This accomplished, he went on board the *Huron* which sailed for Canton on October 27th. In three weeks he was once more in China.

His voyage to date had been a financial disappointment.

Instead of the handsome fortune he had hoped for, he had not even made enough to settle his debts for his cargo. So on credit he decided to purchase a cargo of tea to be carried by the *Huron* to Hamburg, while he returned to the United States in the summer of 1806. Here more bad news awaited him: he learned that Hudson had failed. Only four of the twenty priests who owed him money had honored their notes and Hudson had returned home a year before to die. Also he and Cleveland were now certain that Rouissillon was dead and his funds lost. Efforts to collect insurance on the *Lelia Byrd* likewise were a failure. Only the tea which Shaler had sent to Hamburg and the silks which Cleveland had brought home had produced any profit.

These hardy venturers were by no means discouraged and immediately undertook new speculations. They bought a new ship, the one-hundred-seventy-ton *Aspasia,* which Cleveland was to take back to the West Coast of America while Shaler was to return to China. He undertook to act as supercargo for Ingraham, Phoenix and Nixsen of New York, his old firm, on the *General Hamilton.* This voyage brought him to Canton in January, 1807, where he loaded the *Hamilton* with tea. He then returned to the United States only to receive the discouraging news that Cleveland had fallen a victim to British privateers who had unlawfully seized his ship in the West Indies and had stripped him in a corrupt island admiralty court. Also, the *Hamilton* which he had sent to Europe had run afoul of a Dutch embargo and was detained in one of their ports. The efforts of agents to secure the release of the ship were unsuccessful so Shaler determined to go to Europe in the summer of 1808 to look after it himself. Such were the difficulties of neutral commerce with war-torn Europe.

His voyage over was exciting, for the vessel was captured

by the British and taken in to Plymouth. After his release
he spent a delightful winter in Paris, hospitably looked after
by the American minister, General Armstrong, to whom he
had been introduced by De Witt Clinton. In the spring he
went to Holland where he got some settlement for the cargo
of the *Hamilton* and met Cleveland. They were about to
set out upon another joint business venture when another
Napoleonic war came so close to Holland that their hopes
were blasted. They at length returned to the United States
in the fall of 1809.

Shaler was done with commerce. His ambition had soared,
particularly while he was close to the American legation at
Paris. He now aspired to be a diplomat, the consul at Bordeaux. Also the lure of letters had come upon him. He had
burst into print. On his long voyage to Chile and beyond he
had studied Abbe Don J. Ignatius Molina's *The Geographical, Natural and Civil History of Chile* and he and Richard
Alsop had made a translation which had been published in
Middletown, Connecticut, and again in London. Also he had
written up his California voyage and had published it
in the *American Register*. The beauty and fruitfulness of
California had captured his imagination and he became the
first American to record that glowing enthusiasm which is
now notorious. What great possibilities! California was almost entirely undefended, and he was impressed with the
ease with which it might be captured. What a treasure for
an enterprising power! So he made his published account
a thinly veiled suggestion that the United States take this
beautiful province for itself. The United States had recently
acquired Louisiana, why not California?

Shaler thus advertised himself as one of the few men
among his countrymen who knew anything of farther Hispanic America from first-hand observation. Likewise he

had the backing of the powerful De Witt Clinton and his New York political organization. Therefore he went to Washington in February, 1810, with sanguine hopes of securing an official mission in which he could enhance the interests of the United States and do more to spread the gospel of rational liberty.

# 5. Towards the Halls of Montezuma

SHALER found the Madison administration turning its attention to the Spanish-American empire; in fact, Madison had been concerned over it since his days in Jefferson's cabinet. Ever since 1808 when Napoleon forced the Spanish monarch to abdicate, signs of revolt had flared up in the Spanish colonies which could not fail to concern the United States. No one had any clear idea of what was happening, but some hoped for advantage to the United States from the upheaval. Jefferson and Madison had long set their hearts on obtaining Florida and at least part of Texas: in the confusion of rebellion, adjustments might be made in these quarters. Opportunities for trade, hitherto denied by the Spanish, might now be obtained. Most pressing was the fear of British and French aggression. If Napoleon succeeded in controlling Spain, and the revolts were crushed, France might absorb the Spanish-American empire. Great Britain, on the other hand, was the ally of the Spanish patriotic junta, which was fighting Napoleon. As a reward for such aid England might exact a part of the American estate. Either eventuality would bring these powers too near to the United States. The Spanish colonies might become independent, well and good; but they must never become French or British.

Jefferson and Madison had suffered much from Napoleon and John Bull since 1805, but 1810 found Great Britain less exasperating, and Madison had a short period of confidence.

He was ready to advance American interests to the south, perhaps to promote Jefferson's idea of Pan-America. In May, 1810, he decided to send trusted and informed agents to watch affairs in Buenos Aires, Caracas, and Vera Cruz, disguised as agents for seamen and commerce. William Shaler, who was acquainted with Robert Smith, Secretary of State, was chosen for the last-named post. But how could he get to Vera Cruz? No American official would be tolerated until the revolutionaries gained control of the port; so a subterfuge was adopted. Since 1781, American agents had been permitted to live in Havana, unofficially. Just at the moment none was there; so Shaler would go thither—ostensibly as American agent for seamen at that port. He had a second commission as agent, and a third as consul at Vera Cruz, but these must be held in reserve. Meanwhile in Havana he was to await a favorable opportunity to get into Mexico as soon as the revolution obtained any measure of success. Shaler was eager for this opportunity to advance liberty, and perhaps his own fame and fortune as well.

He was given full oral and written instructions. He was to assure the Latin Americans of the good will of the government of the United States but by no means should he permit himself to interfere in local affairs or to encourage any armament against Spain, with whom the United States was at peace. He was instructed carefully that the boundaries of his country included Texas and West Florida but he might assure Mexicans that such matters could be easily adjusted with a friendly sister republic such as Mexico might become. Most important, he was to make it plain to whatever authorities he met, that the United States would not permit any Spanish territory to come under the sway of any other power. If danger of encroachment arose, the United States would extend help and protection. He

might "feel the pulse of Cuba as to an estimate of the inducements to . . . incorporation of that island with the
United States in comparison with those of an adherence to
the Spanish Main." Furthermore, he was to obtain information about conditions in Santa Fé and Peru and might
even travel thither. It was a very broad commission.

Shaler arrived in Cuba in the summer of 1810 only to be
met by disappointment. The Captain-General would not
recognize him, and the news from Mexico was bad. Evidently he must stay in Havana as unobtrusively as possible
and content himself with observing. The Secretary had instructed him to write, and he gladly obeyed. Mr. Shaler
liked to write, and many an hour he employed between
meals at Mrs. Scott's boarding house filling sheets with a
handwriting so small and neat that it gave little indica-
tion of the man with his striking figure, tall and domineer-
ing, emphasized by a piercing eye and an impressive manner.

In sleepy Havana he found much to interest him. The
town itself, built on a three-coved bay, guarded by forbidding fortresses and a wall, stretched across a tongue of
land to the sea. Within the wall between the bay and the
ocean the streets were crowded and narrow, lined with
myriads of buildings of no particular character which
housed a motley population, half of whom were Negroes.
Beyond the walls were some rambling suburbs stretched
out in bad order. All told there were one hundred thousand
souls in the town and environs. The center of state and
Church were La Fuerza and the Plaza de Armas, near
which were grouped the limestone cathedral and the government buildings, more substantial than attractive. The
better homes were likewise unattractive to the eye of the

passer-by, but the interiors surrounding the patios often possessed an unexpected elegance and comfort.

The streets were narrow and filthy. Paving stones had to be transported from Mexico and were therefore costly; many byways had no surfacing except mahogany logs, which might far better have been used for furniture. Mud or dust was the pedestrian's portion, and the streets were so narrow and the sugar-carters so insolent that those on foot were jostled, pushed to the walls, and splashed and plastered with dirt. Even more unpleasant was the lack of any system of sewage or garbage disposal; the street was the final resting place of all kinds of waste—a state of affairs which would seem even more disgusting to us than it did to Shaler. Added to this was the stench of *tasajo*— the salted meat which was the main food of the Negroes and poor white people. All streets, however, were not narrow: the Alameda and the *paseo* without the walls were faint foretastes of the Prado and the Malecon. Across the bay, too, on the hills overlooking the harbor, were many pleasant villas where the more fortunate inhabitants might escape the heat and the recurring epidemics of yellow fever. Occasional avenues of royal palms did more than anything else to contribute to what little beauty the city could boast.

Cuban society was in a sad state. "The proud Spaniard" from Europe still strutted in all "the fancied superiority of birth and office," controlling absolutely the offices and preferment of the island. On the other hand, the creoles, or Cuban-born Spaniards, while they made up the bulk of the wealthy commercial and planter class, were given little opportunity for political responsibility. Shaler thought them idle, dissipated, badly educated, with a perpetual grievance against the Spaniards. A more "vile and depraved populace," he thought, could not exist anywhere. Assassination and robbery were common; hardly a day passed without some atrocity. Shaler found it extremely dangerous to venture out after dark unarmed. Corruption, he believed, pervaded all ranks, for officialdom literally lived on public plunder. In fine, the population was emotional and unstable and so ignorant that Shaler feared that it was utterly incapable of self-government. There seemed little hope of revolution or the spread of rational liberty. The power of the Spanish officials was stronger than anywhere else in the American empire, and Cuba would be the last of the colonies to seek freedom. The few among the creoles who looked for a change thought rather of the rule of some foreign prince, backed by England; they were not republican.

Very discouraging was the contempt in which the United States seemed to be held, and the faith with which the Cubans looked to Great Britain, the ally of the Spanish junta, was even more disconcerting. In the event of war between the United States and Great Britain, Shaler feared that the Cubans, contemptuous of American naval strength, would openly favor England. Such an outcome would be very harmful to the thriving trade which American merchants enjoyed with the island. Not less than 85,000 barrels of flour were needed by Cuba annually, and lumber as well, for boxing sugar. The British had found they could not compete with American prices and had abandoned the field to the United States. American vessels, therefore, kept Cuba supplied and carried away her exports. Shaler himself dabbled a little in this trade—unofficially, of course. His predecessors had been more interested in their own mercantile ventures than in caring for stranded seamen and had destroyed what little prestige the office of agent might have enjoyed. But it was this trade that gave Shaler his only encouragement. Commerce with the United States was resented by the local merchants, who wished to have complete control of both imports and exports. On the other hand, the planters welcomed Yankee trade because it brought goods at lower prices than monopolizing merchants would ever fix.

The creole planting group had shown an interest in Shaler as soon as he arrived. Their leader was Don Francisco Arango, who dominated the *consulado,* or board of trade, and was the chief opponent of the Captain-General and his Spanish followers. Arango and his associates were planning to secure some sort of home rule and freedom from Spanish appointees. Very shortly after Shaler landed, Arango sent Don Antonio del Valle Hernandez, secretary of the *consulado,* to talk with Shaler, and several of the planters extended him hospitality, notably a Mr. Fellowes, who entertained him occasionally on his plantation. Shaler thought that in these creoles was the only hope of a move for improving the interests of the United States in Cuba. When the fall of 1810 brought encouraging news of revolution in Santa Fé, Peru, Mexico, and West Florida, with a climax in Cuba itself, Shaler began to work. In October there was a slight outbreak on the island—hardly more than a prematurely discovered plot—when the United States "freed" and annexed West Florida. Taking advantage of the discussion caused by these events, Shaler ventured to broach the subject of revolution to his new-found Cuban friends.

Shaler was very tentative in his approach, so he reported to the State Department, and the response to the suggestion that revolution might bring liberty and better government was not very encouraging. His Cuban acquaintances were distrustful of the ability of the islanders to govern themselves; moreover, a new *cortes* had just been established by those who were trying to drive Napoleon out of Spain, and promised reforms. Cuba was sending a delegate to this body armed with a long memorial, the handiwork of Arango and his friends in the *consulado*. They had described at length the abuses in Cuba and had petitioned for autonomy and the reorganization of the Spanish-American empire into a kind of federation of provinces. Shaler was shown this document and had, perforce, to be content until the *cortes* had received and acted on the petition. The response was not what had been expected. Instead of the reform petitioned for, came rumors of a change which to the Cubans was truly shocking. In May, 1811, it was reported that the *cortes* was planning to abolish slavery.

Such a possibility filled the ruling class with consternation; they depended upon slave labor for wealth and comfort. In their wrath and perplexity the leaders summoned an extraordinary *cabildo* and uttered flaming words. Proposals were made for immediate administrative independence from the Spanish regency, qualified by a protestation of eternal loyalty to the deposed king. It was all talk at the time, for nothing was done, but some of the influential people had begun to take a new line of thought. Within a few days, Don Joseph Arango, cousin of Don Francisco and former treasurer of the island, came to Shaler with an unexpected suggestion.

His associates realized, he said, that the Spanish patriotic junta was just a tool of the British and they feared that Cuba might soon become an English colony. Such a prospect was unpleasant in the extreme to the Arangos and their planter friends because of English hostility to the slave trade. "Now," said Arango, "there is really but one course for us to take, which is, to solicit a union with you and become one of your confederated states." Shaler replied that the United States was ever ready "to promote the most intimate relations of friendship" with the island. He brought out some copies of the federal and state constitutions as well as the journal of the Continental Congress to show Arango how the United States had harmonized the interests of slave and free states. Now something might be done. But the flame of interest died down as quickly as it had flared up. The creoles relapsed into indifference. Shaler feared more than ever the increasing influence of Great Britain which boded no good to the United States, living under the shadow of impending war with that government.

The days of his Cuban sojourn were numbered by the troubled state of island politics. When Napoleon had invaded Spain, the Cubans had patriotically turned on the French planters in Cuba and sequestered their property. The Spanish officials expected eventually to dispose of these plantations to their own enrichment. Now the junta sent orders in September, 1811, to restore their estates to such of the French as had been naturalized. Peculating Spanish officials were furious at the loss of this prize; while their enemies, the Spanish creole planters, rejoiced, for they sympathized with their French associates and had no wish to see officialdom any richer. The Spanish rulers, egged on by the clerical hierarchy who hated French freethinking, now began a drive to expel foreigners, especially the French. Shaler's old French sympathies were well known, and the Captain-General probably saw a good excuse to get rid of the agent who was friendly with the Arango party. Shaler lived in expectation of some hostile act, but as usual nothing happened at once, and he went off to Fellowes' plantation for a visit.

While he was there, the blow fell. On November 8th, he was arrested and carried back to Havana before the Captain-General. The Marqués de Someruelos was not at his ease, for he was a timid little fat man who wished to be honest. He was polite, almost apologetic, but with devious twistings and turnings in halting French indicated that Shaler had stayed much too long. Shaler protested, also in French—as his Spanish had not yet reached the stage of fluent speech—but had to be satisfied with a left-handed sort of apology for the unceremonious arrest. Before he left the presence, however, he made an attempt to advance his pet project.

"I took advantage of the occasion to insinuate that I was able to meet His Excellency on higher ground than I had yet appeared to stand on." He explained that the United States would never permit Cuba to become the property of any other nation—that if the Captain-General saw any danger of that, he might appeal to the American government for aid and protection. Between the lines one reads that he hinted at the idea of union with the United States to be arranged between the Marqués and the consul-designate. Someruelos seemed not a whit surprised; in fact he had heard something of the same thing before—from Wilkinson, in 1809. He expressed a desire for continued friendship with the United States but would make no other comment; he was not going to commit himself, we may suspect, to this intimate of his enemies, the Arangos. Shaler bowed himself out.

He must leave, he knew, but he would not depart with undignified haste. He busied himself in preparing an extensive report on the possibilities of independence and compiled a descriptive list of the men who might be interested; in due course these papers were pigeonholed in the State Department. Opportunely enough, he received a letter from New Orleans reporting that a "Colonel Bernard" had arrived there from Mexico, delegated by the province of Colonia, to seek arms, money, and friends in the United

States. "Colonel Bernard" was optimistic about success in Mexico and was eager to get in touch with Shaler. The latter, therefore, decided to go to New Orleans and attempt contact with the Mexican patriots.

Before his final departure he had further conference with del Valle Hernandez, who confided to him the Arango plan for Cuban independence, constitution and all. Del Valle Hernandez also gave him a curious memorandum to be sent to Washington. This statement disclosed the fear of the creoles, that in case of a war between Great Britain and the United States their island would either become British or suffer disastrously from a blockade. Rather than endure British rule the creoles wished to declare themselves independent, but where could they get arms and other aid? The memorandum went on to say, perhaps for purposes of dissimulation if any mischance befell the letter, that the United States presumably would be too weak to be of much help. Evidently the Arango party hoped, in case of British menace, for some sort of independence or autonomy maintained under the protection of the United States.

Shaler assured del Valle Hernandez that "Your friends should rely with confidence on the American people, we are able to support and protect you in all cases, if you are true to yourselves. You will see the storm approach when you should loose [sic] no time in sending a confidential agent to Washington." He arranged with his interlocutor for a continued correspondence with him to and from New Orleans. Shaler had made it clear to both factions that Cuba must stay Spanish or become independent and that the island could look to the United States for protection. His confidence in the ability of the Cubans to understand or enjoy rational liberty was perhaps somewhat shaken. On December 11, 1811, he set out for New Orleans to encourage the

Mexican cause, which at last seemed to promise more vigorous action.

Governor Claiborne had many news items for Shaler when he reached New Orleans. Not only were the revolutionary generals, Rayón and Morelos, busy in Mexico, but a filibustering fever had broken out along the northern border. The seat of this epidemic was the "neutral ground" east of the Sabine, a no-man's land since 1806, and a natural haunt of banditti. Some adventurers were organizing a column here to invade Mexico, ostensibly to aid liberty. Shaler further learned that Vera Cruz was cut off from the interior, and that a trade lane had been opened from central Mexico through Texas with its terminus at Natchitoches—Louisiana's western outpost on the edge of the "neutral ground." Trade and revolution thus seemed to center on the frontier and, as Vera Cruz was impossible, Natchitoches seemed to be the place at which to observe events and, perhaps, begin his official mission.

Shaler wrote Washington reporting his purpose to go to the frontier unless instructed to the contrary. As usual, he received no reply to his letter. Monroe had his hands full with the approaching war with Great Britain. England was Spain's ally, and he could not afford to give the British government an excuse for further aggression on the ground that the United States was breaking the rules of neutrality by permitting filibustering expeditions to be organized against Spain. The memory of the West Florida episode was still vivid; it behooved the State Department to be wary. To Shaler this continued silence was very trying, and his spirits sank as low as his fortune—which had recently dropped to almost nothing. His friend Robert Smith was out of favor, and he himself was not certain of Monroe's good will.

A new arrival shortly appeared to rouse Shaler's drooping spirits. José Bernardo Gutiérrez de Lara, generally spoken of as Bernardo, returned from Washington. He it was of whom Shaler had heard in Cuba as "Colonel Bernard," the man who declared himself to be the agent of the unfortunate rebel chieftain, Hidalgo. He had seen Madison and Monroe and now came armed with a letter from John Graham, chief clerk of the State Department, to Governor Claiborne which seemed to give him a slight tinge of official sanction. Claiborne turned him over to Shaler with the advice that the latter pay his expenses from government funds and see that he got to Natchitoches. This charge pleased Shaler, for he found Bernardo "a prudent man, ardent in the cause and possessing a great deal of plain good sense, . . . full of admiration of what he has seen in our country." He feared, however, that the Mexican might fall into other hands, for the French agent at New Orleans and some foreign adventurers seemed to be seeking Bernardo's confidence; in fact, the French agent told Shaler that his government was interested in promoting Spanish-American independence. Shaler was not going to let French influence win Bernardo away from his patronage; so he had the Mexican live with him. While they waited for a barge to take them to Natchitoches, he carefully schooled Bernardo in the true character of all European governments, showing him that the American system was the only one calculated to promote liberty. Bernardo proved an appreciative listener, especially as Shaler was paying his board.

The delayed barge was ready, at length, and on April 8th the voyage began. A voyage, in reality, it was: first two hundred and twenty miles up the Mississippi to the mouth of the Red River and thence two hundred and sixty-six miles to Natchitoches—a trip that was to take twenty days.

Shaler found Natchitoches to be a queer mixture of age

and youth, of bustle and decay, of life and death. The town itself was the oldest settlement in Louisiana, tracing its history back to Spanish days in 1691. Indians, Spanish, and French had all controlled it; now it was American. The French had established and maintained the town on a hill some half a mile from the site of 1812. As the surroundings had become more settled, the farmers had drifted away from it to their plantations, and the traders found the river bank more convenient; so the old site had been abandoned. The village was a patchwork of French, Spanish, Indian, and American. Only five or six of the dwellings were substantial; the rest of the forty or fifty families lived in an odd conglomeration of mean-looking houses on a few streets close to the river, the space for which seemed to be grudged by the forest, scarce several hundred yards beyond. Behind the town on a hill was Fort Claiborne, commanding a fine view up and down stream. The river itself was muddy and temperamental; at times, wicked—at others, scarcely seeming to flow. By its banks were forests of reeds with huge flocks of birds, and its waters teemed with fish. It was a sportsmen's paradise; life was easy, and the inhabitants hoped to keep it so. The leading citizens, Dr. John Sibley, the Indian agent, Judge Carr, the magistrate, Colonel Pike, and the officers at the fort and the merchants and planters welcomed these ambassadors of liberty, and feted them to the limit of their digestions, for Natchitoches tables were famous.

Filibustering was the interest of the moment, and Shaler was beset. The United States was in a precarious international position. War with Great Britain was approaching, and the government could not afford to offend Spain, no matter how interested in liberty her citizens might be. Shaler could not countenance aid to the invaders, but Bernardo, on the other hand, was eager to promote his cause. French influence, here as in New Orleans, sought to gain his ear. American adventurers and Spanish deserters were about in sufficient numbers, and the latter told Bernardo how easy it would be to gain support once he brought a force into Texas. Torn between sympathy and duty, Shaler made concessions to the former at the expense of the latter. In spite of neutrality, perhaps it was "a matter of indispensable necessity to open a communication with the Republicans [in Mexico] . . . to arm them, to organize them, and to put them in a state to resist such an invasion." The best way out of the dilemma was for the War Department to send down an army to guard the frontier, prevent filibustering, and get in touch with Mexico or at least "offer an Assylum [sic] to the fugitives, organize and discipline them."

He kept his eye on Bernardo, who promised to listen to no unneutral proposals without Shaler's permission. He also helped Bernardo write a report to the rebel Mexican commander, General Rayón, describing his favorable reception in the United States, urging him to send a mission to Washington, and declaring it to be the general opinion in the United States that there should be union to expel all European domination. In their spare time, of which they had a great deal, he drew up a scheme of government to guide Bernardo in planning the new republic, and together they kept a little printing press busy. Thus was Bernardo able to send inflammatory proclamations and pamphlets into Mexico.

In reality, Bernardo was deceiving Shaler, for he was plotting with Lieutenant Augustus Magee and some Natchitoches merchants, who wanted to sell supplies, to organize an invasion which Magee was to lead. It was not long before

Shaler discovered it and found in his protégé "a weakness of mind" that he had not suspected before. Bernardo indulged "himself in the most ridiculous flights of vanity" and was furious when he heard that Rayón had established the government which Bernardo had expected to organize. Of his discoveries Shaler gave no hint to his associate: "I intend even to suffer myself to be deceived so far as to advance him [more money] if he requests it." In fact, Shaler himself was in no pleasant position. Those who favored Spain looked upon him as a fomenter of revolution, while the filibustering party considered him a government spy trying to thwart them. Such were the difficulties of official neutrality. Meanwhile he fell sick of the fever.

During Shaler's illness Magee's expedition crossed into Mexico one hundred and thirty strong on August 8th, and two days later Bernardo left Natchitoches to join them, as Shaler reported, "with great reluctance and evidently under the influence of fear." Before going he apologized to Shaler for deceiving him. "I felt myself humiliated for him, at his ill-timed humility, and want of character . . . and determined in my own mind that if he should return to give him no further countenance." His apprehensions, however, were brushed aside by the tide of events. Magee's expedition occupied the Mexican town of Nacogdoches, and the fame of this exploit spread. Numerous Americans drifted over the border and volunteering became a "perfect mania." Business at Natchitoches boomed and two hundred mules were employed constantly in bringing in booty and sending out supplies. Shaler wrote his brother that as Magee had "the fairest prospects of complete success," he hoped that his own diplomatic mission might now have a chance to gain "some lustre" and he looked forward to crossing the border.

He must be discreet, though, and decided to wait until the capital of Texas had been captured.

Early in October, 1812, Shaler had a second visitor, Dr. John H. Robinson, who arrived with a commission of his own. Robinson had been active on the border some half-dozen years before and now he was sent back as agent of friendship to arrange with the Spanish authorities of the northern provinces of Mexico for the exterminating of the filibusters. Monroe hoped his mission would quiet Spanish fears and prevent their officials from aiding the British in the War of 1812. Shaler was to stay at Natchitoches free from any connection with the invaders; while Robinson was to go to the Spanish themselves. Monroe assured Shaler that the new mission was in no way to conflict with or supersede his own. Shaler, however, wondered if Robinson were not sent to promote an annexation scheme similar to that by which the United States had acquired West Florida; such was the suspicion on the border.

Shaler took Monroe's instructions to heart, and when a new complication arose, he acted vigorously. As soon as he heard that Bernardo was attempting to recruit in a village in the neutral ground, he took a detachment of soldiers to prevent it—only to discover that the people of Bayou aux Pierres were not heeding the Mexican's pretensions. Good news followed almost immediately; Magee and Bernardo had captured Goliad (La Bahia).

Bernardo now was in the zenith of exaltation. Texas and Mexico were bound to be free, and he would be the grand ruler. Magnanimously, therefore, he proposed to Shaler the union of the two Americas, his great Mexico and the United States, on condition that Shaler would ever advise him and the United States supply troops. This rosy dream soon became a nightmare, for the Spanish advanced toward

Goliad in force, and Magee collapsed from the effects of some swift illness. He lost his nerve when it was most needed and made a sorry spectacle, urging surrender. The whole enterprise so successfully launched seemed about to break up. At Christmas Shaler was so discouraged that he might have left for home had winter travel not been so difficult.

Spring brought a return of hope. The cards were all reshuffled. Magee died (some said by his own hand), and while Bernardo was trying to gather the reins in his inept hands, new leaders appeared. General John Adair arrived on the scene, Blennerhassett was in the offing, and ghosts of the Burr scheme seemed to be walking once again. The Spaniards, too, contributed to the renewal of hope by giving up the siege of Goliad and retreating. Shaler was fully restored in his faith: "Nothing now prevents me from proceeding on my journey but the fear of being regarded as a partisan in the revolution and thereby committing the government."

Even before he sealed the letter containing these hopeful words, a third visitor appeared. On April 4th, José Alvarez de Toledo arrived at Natchitoches. This native Cuban had been sent as a delegate from Santo Domingo to the Spanish *cortes,* where he had proved too radical for his own good and had retreated to the United States. Here he had gained the reputation of an authority on Hispanic-American revolutionary affairs and had proceeded to meet and dominate Bernardo. They planned that Toledo should liberate Cuba and Haiti while Bernardo was freeing Mexico. The Caribbean situation, however, was inauspicious; so Toledo, seeing Bernardo on the road to success, decided to join him and presented Shaler with an old letter which Monroe had given him when it was thought he was on his way to Cuba. Once more was Shaler convinced by an agent of rational liberty.

Toledo's "candor and honorable views I every day more admire," he reported, and was glad that Toledo's manner obtained for him the "sympathy and respect of the citizens of Natchitoches." Shaler, disgusted with Bernardo, saw in Toledo real hope for success. He defended Toledo against charges when Colonel Nathaniel Cogswell appeared to accuse him and helped him by communicating his distrust of Bernardo's capacity to the Americans in the latter's force. Toledo was the very one to resume Bernardo's expedition and keep it out of Adair's hands.

No sooner had Shaler made the welcome discovery than the lost Robinson appeared. His report added to the waxing enthusiasm. Though his ostensible mission had been a failure, he had got in touch with some of the revolutionaries and had been encouraged by the discovery that many of the subordinates of the Spanish commander, Salcedo, were dissatisfied and would welcome independence. Once the invaders penetrated to the capital of Texas, they would find friends where they might have been least expected. Toledo, Robinson, and Shaler fed one another's enthusiasm. Shaler's chief worry was the dispute between Toledo and Robinson as to how many Americans should be permitted the privilege of aiding in the freeing of Mexico; Toledo feared lest his Anglo-Saxon allies might dominate. Certain plans emerged from their hopeful converse. Toledo would join the invaders; Robinson, ignorant of the fact that Monroe had discharged him, would go to Washington to get help; Shaler would wait. So the trio separated.

Hardly had Toledo left when the great news arrived. Bernardo's force had captured San Antonio, the Texan capital. Shaler now saw his career straight before him, brightly illuminated. He wrote to Robinson asking him to buy him a full uniform at the expense of the State Department so that in his functioning in the new republic of Mexico he might be dressed as befitted the consular representative of the United States. Bernardo forthwith declared Texas independent and assumed the title of governor; Shaler prepared to join him, for success had now made that step proper.

The hopeful consul had still much to learn of the Latin-American temperament. Bernardo was not equal to his task. He massacred captives and otherwise acted so incompetently that Shaler concluded that Toledo must take control; whereupon he backed him determinedly, in spite of various efforts of the creole's enemies to discredit him. Bernardo's disgusted officers finally invited Toledo to take command, and for a little while news was favorable. By July 14th, Shaler was convinced that "verry [sic] little is required to ensure complete success to this revolution, if that little is withheld it must as certainly fail, and . . . involve thousands in the most frightful misery and ruin." Shaler could not keep from doing his bit. On July 20th he set forth to join the triumphal progress. He did not get far, and it was well he did not. In some unexplained way he lost his horses on the road, and had to delay long enough to be overtaken by a despatch from Washington.

The troublous experiences of Madison and Monroe in the discouraging War of 1812 had cured them of whatever enthusiasm and interest they may have had in promoting Latin-American revolutions. Monroe specifically ordered Shaler under date of June 5, 1813:

. . . not to interfere in the affairs of those provinces, or to encourage any armaments of any kind against the existing government. The United States being at peace with Spain wish to preserve that relation with whatever government may exist. This is the spirit of the instructions given you at the commencement of your service, and they have never since been altered.

He was not to proceed to San Antonio without further instructions. Shaler could do nothing, therefore, but return once more to Natchitoches in a disturbed frame of mind to write a long explanation to Monroe. He assured the Secretary that he had taken no official action and had recommended Toledo only in his private capacity.

He still encouraged himself to wait a little longer, as he wrote his brother: "My mind sometimes soars very high and at others falls pretty low. My health is good and my mind quiet. In all other respects I am like a soldier in garrison who has his rations only." He even invited his brother to come West and while visiting him look for a place to settle down. But his hopes were really blasted. Toledo had arrived too late. On August 18th the Spanish defeated the revolutionaries at San Antonio. Toledo fled to the border, and even the optimistic Shaler was convinced that this essay in promoting rational liberty was lost beyond the hope of revival. Late in September he bade final adieu to the lazy little riverside settlement of Natchitoches. The light of Mexican independence had almost gone out and was not to be rekindled for nearly a decade. Shaler was never to reach the halls of Montezuma.

# 6. On the Shores of Barbary

THE "dark continent" of Africa like the other mysterious regions of the eighteenth century claimed a share of Yankee ingenuity. The first agents of the United States to go thither were neither explorers nor trade promoters, rather they were ministers of punishment. The flag of the new republic had been fouled with insult and American citizens had been held in slavery by pirates putting out from African ports. Various agents had been sent there unsuccessfully to right these wrongs but it was to be William Shaler who was to succeed in the difficult task.

On the southern shores of the Mediterranean sprawled the four Barbary kingdoms. Algiers, Morocco, Tripoli, and Tunis were ruled by Turkish military chieftains whose main interest and principal support was piracy. For years these Moslem marauders had preyed upon the Mediterranean commerce of Christian nations and when the United States came into being, the new republic found its infant commerce likewise beset. Algerine corsairs immediately began to harry American merchantmen and the Tripolitans finally drove the United States into war, 1801–1805. War with Algeria had been avoided because the United States, before the navy was created, had begun the practice common even among powerful European nations of paying annual tribute to secure immunity.

The humiliation of tribute payments was resented in the United States but for some years there seemed to be no help for it. The dangers and perplexities which beset Jefferson and Madison during the confusions of the Napoleonic wars prevented any change. The little effort they could spare was engrossed in the Tripolitan War. By 1812, however, Algerine conditions had become intolerable. The Dey of that country picked a quarrel over the tribute and began piratical attacks upon the merchantmen of the United States within his reach. Only the fact that the War of 1812 drove the flag out of the Mediterranean saved United States shipping from great damage. The Algerine navy only succeeded in capturing one American prize, the *Edwin*, George C. Smith, master, with a crew of ten and a passenger. These unfortunates were thrown into slavery and their government was unable even to ransom them. While the war lasted, Madison and Monroe could do nothing, but they were determined that here was a score to be settled at the first opportunity.

The Algerine question was first on the agenda when the ink had dried on the Treaty of Ghent. President Madison promptly asked Congress to declare war on February 23, 1815, and by March 2nd the declaration was proclaimed. A naval expedition was speedily organized and plans made to send with it a commission of three, two naval officers and a civilian, with power to negotiate for a peace.

While these preparations were in progress, William Shaler appeared in Washington to seek a new opportunity to advance his country's interests. He was now richer in diplomatic experience than he had been when in Louisiana. In fact, he had turned from his great objective of promoting the cause of rational liberty and, fired by the flames of the War of 1812, he had been working to advance national power. He had become ambitious to engage in statecraft and to further the interests of the nation by playing a part in world politics.

Even while he was in Louisiana he had been working on such plans. He was appalled by the seemingly irresistible advance of Napoleon and the annihilation of the balance of power. Something must be done to resist the conqueror's demands and to restore the balance. So he proposed that the United States and Great Britain cease fighting each other, unite to create a new world order "and give peace to mankind." Likewise such a plan would aid in the establishment of the republics he had tried to help create in Latin America. He proposed a redrawing of boundaries, a reapportioning of territory and the organizing of new states.

There were to be four republics, the first was to be made from Central America and Mexico, the second from New Granada and Quito, the third from Peru, the fourth from Buenos Aires and Chile. The British Empire was to receive Puerto Rico, Santo Domingo, the Philippine Islands, and the northern portion of Brazil including the Amazon Valley. The United States was to absorb Cuba, Florida, Nova Scotia and Canada. The new states and the United States and Great Britain were to unite in a "grand confederation on principles best calculated to insure their own happiness and peace to the world." He proposed these boundaries to "remove forever every political jealousy." England he felt could not object to surrendering Canada because his proposals would give complete security to her possessions in the East and West Indies, and besides she would soon undoubtedly obtain such items as Cyprus, Candia, Sicily, Sardinia, the Belearic Islands, the Azores, and the Canaries at Napoleon's defeat. Such generous accessions would prevent her from missing Canada and Nova Scotia. All members of the confederation should agree to no separate peace except by common consent.

A memorandum outlining this plan had been transmitted by Shaler to the State Department on August 1812 where it was promptly pigeonholed. But it represented a definite interest which he was cultivating; he was looking for a chance to extend his country's power by diplomacy. When he reached home from the Mexican border, late in 1813, he had next obtained a tantalizing opportunity which he undertook with the hope that it would give him an opportunity for further diplomatic preferment.

In January, 1814, shortly after Shaler reported to Madison, there appeared to be a possibility of peace. President Madison received assurances that negotiations would be agreed to. He therefore sent a commission to a suggested neutral point, Gothenburg, Sweden, to await the completion of arrangements for a meeting with British plenipotentiaries. As Napoleon's defeat at Leipzig made a general peace conference probable, a new need for an agent presented itself. The Anglo-American peace discussions and those of the European conference would both concern the United States. Maritime rights, "free ships, free goods," the disposition of American territory, particularly that of Spain, and the slave trade would all be on the agenda. Madison and Monroe knew that they must keep the Anglo-American conference aware of what was transpiring at the projected general congress. They decided therefore to appoint Shaler to accompany the American Commissioners to their headquarters and then to proceed to the general conference with sufficient diplomatic standing to gain information of the deliberations of the larger body. He was designated a bearer of dispatches at $2,000 a year and was to be on call by the peace commissioners to undertake such confidential missions as they might find desirable.

Three of the proposed members of the commission, John Quincy Adams, James A. Bayard and Albert Gallatin, were already in Europe working on arrangements for a conference, so the remaining commissioners, Henry Clay and Jonathan Russell, sailed with Shaler to Gothenburg. Shortly after their arrival in April, the two commissioners sent Shaler to Amsterdam to summon Bayard and Gallatin to Sweden and then on to Paris with dispatches for William H. Crawford, U.S. Minister there. He was also to observe the treaty negotiations then going on at the French capital. He was there when the agreement was reached May 30, 1814, and then rejoined the commissioners who assembled in Ghent in July. Here he served as a confidential assistant to the secretary of the commission, Christopher Hughes, Jr., during the early stages of these tortuous negotiations.

When the expected general Congress assembled at Vienna in September, Shaler was not sent thither. The probable reason was the unfortunate state of the nerves of the commission. By that time, Adams, Gallatin and Bayard were at loggerheads with Clay and Russell and agreement on anything was difficult. When it was proposed to send Shaler, who had been closely associated with Clay and Russell, Adams and his associates refused almost automatically— no creature of Clay and Russell should represent the commission. He was likewise excluded from the confidential work which he had hitherto aided. John Quincy Adams recorded that he had developed an undue sense of his own importance and had become arrogant and indiscreet, though Adams was not charitable towards anything or anyone connected with Clay at Ghent.

Shaler considered this action as an insult to his integrity

and he asked to be allowed to return to the United States. The speedy granting of his request further disgruntled him and he left in anger. His difficulties probably arose more from the bickerings within the commission than from any particular fault of his. Despite this bitterness the experience had not been wholly unsatisfactory, he had gained a wide acquaintance in diplomatic circles and the friendship of Clay and particularly Jonathan Russell was to be long-lived and satisfying.

It thus transpired that he returned to Washington just as Madison and Monroe were looking for a civilian to complete the peace commission at Algiers. Shaler himself was anxious for another assignment to Spanish America where he might aid the cause of liberty, but his superiors saw in him other potentialities. Madison invited him to undertake this peace mission and then to settle in Algiers as consul general for all the Barbary states. He accepted and prepared to demand the respect of American power from behind the guns of a fleet in a region ne'er blessed by a single ray from the sun of liberty. He entered upon his new assignment with great enthusiasm. To him it was "an employment very distinguished in itself, surrounded with all 'the pomp and glorious circumstance of war'; and in many respects more agreeable than anything at this time in the gift of the government." It was his hope that the United States might "have a controlling aim in the general affairs of the civilized world" before he died.

Squadrons were organized under two great captains, Stephen Decatur and William Bainbridge. It was with the former that Shaler sailed on the *Guerrière* on May 20, 1815. The commissioners were instructed to make an honorable peace and a treaty which would free the prisoners and relieve the United States from further tribute. However, the

United States was to give voluntarily as much money as either Britain or France agreed to continue. While there was to be no stipulated ransom paid for the prisoners, a private gratuity might be presented afterwards. The commission was provided with $30,000 for the expense of the negotiation, and among the presents they were to take was a beautiful saber for the Dey, which had been secured in London at a cost of $5,000.

On the long voyage of nearly a month Shaler was busy making plans. Desiring to secure publicity in Europe for the fleet's display of American strength, he wrote a series of letters to diplomats and agents of his acquaintance. He asked them to see that the European press printed accounts of the expedition and its full naval strength, so that the powers might be impressed by the rapidity of American recovery from the War of 1812. Not until after the fleet had sailed from Gibraltar in mid-June did it see action.

Shortly after leaving this haven the squadron encountered an Algerine frigate of forty-six guns which the *Guerrière* immediately engaged. The battle lasted a brief twenty minutes, during which not an Algerine shot struck the American ship. To Shaler it "resembled a sham fight more than anything else." A few days later a brig of twenty-two guns was captured under circumstances that were later to cause much trouble. These prizes were taken into the Spanish port of Carthagena where it was learned that the grand admiral of Algiers had been killed in the battle. Since they also learned that the Algerine fleet was away from the city, they realized that the opportune time to present their demands was at hand. The fleet sailed immediately, reaching its destination on June 28th, while the Algerines were still uncertain as to the fate of their ships. Under these auspicious circumstances Decatur and Shaler prepared to negotiate.

Since Tobias Lear, Shaler's predecessor, had found the Swedish Consul, Johann Norderling, most helpful, Monroe had instructed the commission to work through him. When the Swedish ensign and a white flag were hoisted on the *Guerrière,* Norderling and the Algerine captain of the port came on board. The latter was dumfounded to learn of the capture of the war vessels and immediately asked for a truce while negotiations were pending, for he feared that the remainder of the Algerine fleet might return at any time and be captured by the American expedition. Decatur and Shaler not only refused the truce, but also a request that the negotiations be conducted on shore—the treaty was to be made aboard the *Guerrière.*

These demands were transmitted to the Dey, who, having no option in the matter, consented, and the next day his representative appeared on board the flagship. Captain Decatur and Shaler presented a draft treaty which they demanded should be signed immediately. This treaty, as Monroe had instructed, contained no references to tribute nor to presents; such payments the American Commissioners declared would never again be formally agreed to by the United States. But, they added, the United States was a magnanimous and generous nation and would give presents on occasion. The Algerine representative made various attempts to bargain, but received only one concession. As the war vessels just captured by Decatur were in poor condition and would require a large expenditure to fit them for a voyage to America, the commissioners agreed to return them, although such a stipulation was not included in the treaty. Finally, the emissary of the Dey was ordered to take the treaty ashore and to bring it back signed. Until this was done there would be no truce, and the Algerine fleet might sail into the trap at any moment. Despite the fact that the distance to shore was five miles, the treaty was signed and returned in three hours—none too soon, as it happened, for immediately thereafter one of the Algerine vessels hove in sight.

By July 4th the formalities had been completed, and Shaler went ashore, where he was introduced to the Dey, to whom he presented the ceremonial sword. He also dispersed some $17,000 among myriad officials, including the Dey's barber and two cooks. Thus Shaler entered upon the duties of his new position as Consul General to the Barbary states, with general oversight of the activities and expenditures of the American consuls at Tripoli, Tunis and Morocco.

Shaler found his new post a strange, unreal sort of place. Algiers was impressive, unlike anything most Americans knew. The city itself was located on a semicircular bay twelve to fifteen miles wide, rising from the sea and stretching out on the sides of a steep amphitheater. It was a walled city, shaped like a topsail, compactly filled with 50,000 people living in square, whitewashed houses. Its narrow streets were steep, seldom wide enough to permit carts to pass, all seeming to lead to the fortress or *Casauba* which dominated the city. The houses were flat with roofs protected by parapets. There were no windows on the street, and the long and narrow rooms were built around interior courts. The metropolis was heavily guarded, fortified with a thousand pieces of heavy cannon, and the gates of the city were closed each night.

Shaler in time rented one of these square houses from the heirs of a murdered Dey for $250 a year. Two sides of his house looked out over the sea and had a terrace from which he might enjoy the chance sight of an American ship entering the harbor. He could not, however, fly his flag from his house; it was a violation of Moslem religious custom to permit a foreign banner in the city. As it was necessary to display a flag as a sign of peace to assure incoming vessels that the harbor was safe to enter, Shaler, like the other consuls, hired a garden outside the city where he could fly the Stars and Stripes, protected by a soldier whom he had engaged.

His household was small, for he was a confirmed bachelor —though one with a roving eye. He had brought with him his nephew and namesake, William Shaler, and during the early years of his stay, William Buell, a young man in ill health, served as his secretary. As was customary, he employed a native factotum or dragoman, Baptiste Jolí, and various other servants. It was necessary that he constantly distribute largesse. Whenever he landed or boarded a boat, he was saluted with five guns, for which he had to pay forty dollars. Whenever American vessels arrived in the harbor and remained more than three days, a present of bullocks, poultry, bread, fruits and vegetables was sent on board, for which the Consul had to pay fourteen dollars. Life was made up of paying for presents. However, his salary of $4,000 was ample to support a style of luxury which he described as "splendid and elegant, but entirely unencumbered with fastidious and fatiguing forms." In fact, his social opportunities were limited, because his relationships with the Turkish rulers were confined to official business. He and his fellow consuls were consequently thrown much into each other's company, and they formed a society which Shaler found "most friendly and pleasing." His closest ties were with the Swedish consul and, in later times, with the Danish and the Dutch representatives. Although his relations with the British were to be friendly and fateful, he unfortunately found little reason to like the French.

The government with which he had to deal was a peculiar one. The kingdom of Algiers was a fief of the Turkish Empire and was ruled by a military force of some four thousand Janissaries from Turkey. All administrative posts were held by the officers of this alien force. The Dey, or *Bashaw,* was elected from among them by the *Divan,* or Council, composed of present and former corps commanders. These elections were ratified by the Turkish Emperor. The Dey appointed his ministers from the *Divan,* including the *Hasnagee* (minister of finance and interior), the *Aga* (war minister), the *Vikel Argee* (minister of marine and foreign affairs) and two others. The Dey and these ministers were the government and ruled unchecked, except by the fear of revolt among the Janissaries. These revolts were apt to occur at any moment—once, in fact, there were seven during a single day. When Shaler began his consulship, Omar was the Dey, but Shaler was to see several successors within his years of service.

This Turkish government ruled a mixed people. The largest group were the Moors, who were predominant in the cities. There were also Arabs, Biscaries, Mozabis, Kabyles and the Touariks; in Algiers alone there were 5,000 Jews. The Moors themselves were a mixed race of the ancient inhabitants, Mohammedan conquerors, Turks and emigrants from Spain. The Arabs were plainsmen, descendants of the Mohammedan invaders who had swept in from Asia in the seventh century. The Biscaries were related to the Arabs, and all spoke Arabic in some form. The other three groups were probably descended from the original African inhabitants, and spoke a language which was distinct. These people were eventually to be of great interest to Shaler.

While becoming acquainted with the North African people and their customs, Shaler found his diplomatic duties difficult and dangerous. He found himself early on his own, for Decatur did not remain long, taking his fleet to

Tunis and Tripoli. To be sure, Bainbridge arrived not long afterwards, but after displaying his forces to the Dey, he also went on to impress the Tripolitans and Tunisians. These visits concluded the tour of African duty of the fleet, and, according to orders, most of the war vessels returned to America leaving only a frigate and two sloops in the Mediterranean under Captain Shaw. Even before Bainbridge left, however, Shaler discovered that his position was none too secure.

The first trouble arose from the agreement to return the two warships which the squadron had captured on its way to Algiers. This concession had been made at Decatur's insistence and against Shaler's better judgment. Indeed, there had been friction between the two men at every step. Decatur was overbearing, and was inclined to run things without too much deference to his civilian associate, thus earning from Norderling the title "Bashaw Decatur," as he strutted about sporting the Order of the Cincinnati. The captain, although he insisted upon the return of the ships, did not wait to see that transaction consummated. Shaler thought that he should have brought the boats to Algiers before sailing for home. Actually, Decatur did no more than take an Algerine captain to Spain and secure the transfer to him. No sooner had Decatur departed than Spain refused to let the Algerine brig sail.

The difficulty lay in the fact that Decatur's capture of the brig had been irregular. He had pursued it into Spanish waters where it had run on a shoal; it had then been seized in violation of international law. Decatur's excuse was that the brig lay among shoals which he could not blockade, and that she would undoubtedly slip away at high water in the night. Since she was provisioned for a long voyage of depredation, he had decided to stop her. Spain, however, refused to recognize Decatur's claim, as Shaler and the Algerine authorities learned when the frigate returned on July 23rd without the brig. The Dey lost little time in making sharp demands upon the American consul, even insisting that if Spain did not surrender the brig, the United States must supply one in its place.

The Consul was in a difficult position. He was far from home and without instructions. In writing to Secretary Monroe of his difficulties, Shaler requested authority to secure aid from Captain Shaw in bringing about a settlement. But there was no way of telling when he might receive a reply; the Consul was almost completely cut off from his home government. There was no mail or dispatch service of any kind, and he had to depend upon the accidental opportunities presented by the visit of a war vessel or the sailing of a captain whom he could trust. Such procedure was irregular and uncertain, for even American naval officers were careless about forwarding his dispatches and his letters often lay for long periods at various ports, while waiting for ships bound to America.

Shaler was further hampered by financial difficulties. Word of this dilemma reached the Dey's ears, making him disdainful of American resources. Shaw was short of money with which to supply his fleet, and this curtailed his cruising range. On the other hand Shaler, Decatur, and Bainbridge had been entrusted with $30,000 deposited with Baring Brothers which could be drawn on order of two of the commissioners. Before Decatur left, he and Shaler had drawn half of this for Shaler's use. He now advanced some of these funds for Shaw's needs, but when this expedient became known, the Algerines became contemptuous of American poverty. The Dey came to enjoy the idea that the American demonstration of the previous year was a feverish and unusual burst of strength which could not be maintained by a weak, poverty-stricken, and very distant power.

Under these circumstances, the Consul General found it extremely difficult to establish the respect and maintain the prestige which he felt was due his government. As the United States did not pay tribute and as he was not in business and had no favors to dispense, it was not easy for Shaler to create influence. He was determined, however, and overlooked no opportunity to assert his rights. When he found that Turkish soldiers were taking fruits, flowers, and vegetables from his garden outside the city walls, he made the strongest efforts to redress this wrong. After several fruitless protests, he declared to the Dey that he would consider such pilfering a national insult; this threat brought results.

Furthermore, Shaler was determined to forestall any retaliatory raids upon American commerce while the Algerine rage over the loss of the brig was hot. The Consul boldly threatened the Dey with naval might if any harm came to American shipping. He declared that Algerine vessels must bear an American passport or else be in danger of seizure by the American navy. These passports were issued to the native shipmasters for each voyage, a measure by which Shaler sought to impress upon the Algerines that any interference with American vessels would cancel his protection and leave them to the mercies of the American navy. He was particularly insistent upon enforcing respect, because he had discovered that the Algerines often brought in vessels and then let them go, just to show their power. Even the British, Shaler believed, tolerated this practice. But not he. He told the Minister of Marine that any such treatment of American merchantmen would mean reprisals upon the Algerine navy. His attitude in those early days of his mission was belligerent. As he wrote Shaw, "We must fix upon something as near to what is just as we can and browbeat them into its acceptance. Indeed the only way to deal with these people is to treat them as you would plantation Negroes."

The controversy over the brig held by the Spanish came to a partial settlement before Shaler could hear from Monroe and without a call upon Shaw's little fleet. On March 17, 1816, a Spanish flotilla came into port bringing the disputed brig which was to be returned conditionally. In December, a Spanish war vessel had foundered on the Barbary shore; Spain was willing to exchange the Algerine prize for this ship. To this proposal the Dey had to agree, although he felt cheated and suspected that the United States had connived with Spain to rob him.

Within a fortnight after this settlement, another diversion occurred which was to have unfortunate consequences upon American interests. The Algerines had been in the habit, during the confusion of the Napoleonic wars, of preying upon the coasts of the Italian states, kidnaping the inhabitants for slaves. Great Britain, on the warpath against the slave trade, had decided to put a stop to this practice. On March 31, 1816, Lord Exmouth arrived with a large British fleet, and soon flattered and persuaded the Dey into making treaties of peace by which the captives were restored to Sardinia and Naples.

During these negotiations, the American squadron put into Algiers on April 3rd. Shaw had received the Decatur-Shaler treaty of the previous year, duly ratified by the United States Senate, and he and Shaler forthwith proceeded to present it to the Dey for an exchange of ratifications. Unfortunately, however, Omar was feeling particularly elated because of Exmouth's visit. He had interpreted it as a compliment to his power and it had given him a new sense of strength. Consequently, when the two Americans appeared before him, he immediately demanded the President's views regarding the Spanish prize. Shaler explained that the ship bearing the treaty had left the United States before the Consul's request for instruction had been received. The Dey was then brought to discuss the treaty, and produced his copy which was not the same as that just ratified. Evidently, the Algerine minister had inserted some provision relating to indemnity for sailors captured in the war vessels. "This interview terminated by mutual professions of friendly disposition but without the confidence necessary to give any value to such professions." Next day the treaty was returned to Shaler unratified.

"The reasons which they gave for it were probably true," Shaler reported, for in all likelihood no such formality had ever been practiced before. "The treaties existing between foreign powers and Algiers," as far as Shaler knew, were nothing more than capitulations. The return of the treaty caused the naval commanders to talk of war; Captain Oliver Hazard Perry read Roman history to learn how Rome had fought against Carthage. Shaler, however, was opposed to force, despite renewed insults from the Algerines which, he declared, forced him to retire to shipboard. He was therefore relieved when this move proved effective. After some delay, the Swedish Consul Norderling reported that the Dey was much surprised that Shaler had left. He wanted only peace. Negotiations began again, and it was finally agreed that the Dey would write to President Madison directly, in the meantime observing the treaty until a reply was received. This letter was duly prepared in Turkish and addressed to his Majesty, the Emperor of America. In it the Dey declared that as the ships had not been returned the treaty was broken and of no effect. He now proposed that they go back to the original treaty under which the United States paid tribute. He also requested that Shaler be removed as soon as possible. The Consul suspected that these proposals were made because the Dey did not believe the United States could muster sufficient force to support its demands. At any rate, there was to be further delay. Shaw and his fleet sailed off, the Commander having sent Shaler a cask of old whisky as a farewell gift.

There now ensued another long period of waiting during the slow transport of dispatches. The British, however, varied its monotony by providing an exciting summer. In May, Exmouth returned with new demands that excited the wrath of Omar, and insults were exchanged. The British Consul was arrested, and his wife and children unceremoniously hustled about. The Dey also captured British subjects engaged in coral fishing under his license, and in the mêlée some of them were killed. For the time being, this quarrel was smoothed over by presents and meaningless exchanges.

Shaler was naturally a close observer of the episode and, in particular, of the plight of the British Consul, Hugh McDonnell. There were two reasons for deep interest on his part. First, he liked McDonnell and his family. The Consul he recognized as a "strong John Bull but an honorable man," with whom he lived "upon most friendly terms." More particularly, however, Shaler was interested in protecting the dignity of the consular position. He was disappointed in the outcome, which only increased his contempt for British policy. It was his belief that the British had an interest in maintaining the Barbary pirates who conveniently kept down the profits of commercial rivals in the Mediterranean.

Great Britain, however, did not intend to overlook the Dey's insults. Making common cause with the Dutch, whom

Shaler had expected to strike before this, the British ministry sent a joint fleet under Exmouth to inflict punishment. Word of the approach of this armament came from France in July, and when a British war vessel appeared, to take away the British Consul on August 3rd, the Algerines knew what was coming. They sought to prevent the departure of McDonnell, whose wife and daughter were smuggled on board disguised as midshipmen. When this was discovered, the Consul and some British officers and sailors on shore were arrested. Such was the state of affairs when Lord Exmouth's fleet arrived on August 27, 1816. Exmouth demanded the release of the hostages, and when it was refused opened up a bombardment. The fleet threw in 30,000 shots and 300 shells. Hardly a house went undamaged, and the Algerine navy and merchant marine were severely crippled. By the next afternoon the Algerines surrendered.

Shaler had been a witness to all this. During the battle many Turks, probably skulkers, constantly passed in and out of his house, breathing vengeance particularly upon the British Consul upon whom they blamed their woes. From his roof he could see hundreds running along the seashore under his very walls, many of them slaughtered by the guns of the fleet. By night the upper part of his house was in ruins, for five shells had exploded within its walls. As night fell, he learned that the British Consul had been thrown in a dungeon, loaded with chains. By eleven, the general firing had all but ceased—only an occasional gun was to be heard. At midnight he viewed from his terrace a "peculiarly grand and sublime spectacle." Everything in the port seemed aflame, and two burning vessels were drifting out to sea. At this moment a terrific thunderstorm came up, and in the vivid flashes of lightning he could see the fleet retiring offshore before a land breeze. Occasionally the scream of a shell or the flash of a rocket vied with the thunder and lightning. But the battle was spent. When the British landed in the morning, they found Shaler at breakfast on his terrace, served by frightened servants whom he compelled to wait upon him. The British Consul was rescued from his dungeon and a peace was dictated by Exmouth. The Dey was forced to agree to the abolition of Christian slavery, to restore captives, and to pay back the ransom money received under the recent treaties with Naples and Sardinia.

While Algiers was recovering from this humiliation, Shaler awaited the arrival of his instructions and the answer to the Dey's letter. At length in October, Commodore Isaac Chauncey appeared with a fleet of six vessels. His appearance spread consternation among the Algerines, for so wrecked were their defenses that they could expect nothing but a second chastisement. As Chauncey had no dispatches, Shaler decided to sail with him to Gibraltar to await their arrival. After reassuring the Dey that peace alone was desired and that no punishment would be attempted without due warning, he boarded the flagship and sailed off. On finding no word awaiting him at Gibraltar, Shaler visited Morocco, which was under his general supervision. After concluding a satisfactory inspection there he returned to Gibraltar, still seeking his instructions.

The long period of uncertainty finally came to an end when the *Spark* reached Gibraltar with the long-awaited dispatches. Shaler and Chauncey learned that they had been appointed commissioners to settle all difficulties. The Dey was to be told that the United States had been working to persuade the Spanish to surrender the ships. The United States now demanded that the Algerine government sign a new treaty, only slightly modified. In the preceding document it had been provided that United States prizes might be sold in Algiers, a privilege accorded to no other power. Monroe suspected that this might have aroused British opposition and in order to avoid further hindrance, he was willing to drop the point.

The fleet set sail shortly, and on December 7th arrived off Algiers with all plans made and a formal note ready to be delivered to the Dey. Chauncey and Shaler had originally planned to demand that the negotiations be conducted on the quarter-deck of the *Washington,* but the weather was bad and the fleet could not safely run in and anchor under the guns of the fortifications. In addition, the fleet was short of provisions. It was therefore decided that Shaler should go ashore with the acting chaplain of the *Java,* Charles O. Handy, who was to serve as secretary of the mission. Chauncey in the meantime was to go to Port Mahon, the American fleet rendezvous on the island of Minorca, for provisions. So tempestuous was the weather, however, that Shaler and Handy were prevented from landing for a week; on one wild night the *Spark,* on which they were quartered, nearly foundered in the bay. Had the ship been anchored, it and all on board probably would have been lost.

When Shaler finally got ashore on December 15th, he was met by further delays. The Dey, first of all, made much of Chauncey's absence. He then brought up the old question of the ships and the Spaniards, which he claimed the President had not satisfactorily dealt with in his reply. He even called all the foreign consuls to be present while he raised this issue with Shaler. Shaler, however, refused to discuss the matter further, as the President had spoken officially and finally. Then the Dey made another play for delay. He said it had taken eight months and a day, which he counted off on his fingers, for the President to answer him; he would ask the same privilege of time. Because he had just been through a war, he was not ready to make a treaty. If the United States compelled him to sign, he would break it at the first opportunity. He had entered into one treaty with the United States in good faith, but the complexion of things had changed and difficulties had arisen between the two nations. Shaler then said he would have to consult Chauncey who would return in a few days, a demand which the Dey though unnecessary since Shaler had just certified that he was competent to conduct the negotiation. Shaler demanded ten days and, in effect, threatened war, which finally brought the Dey to agreement.

The following day, however, it became apparent that the monarch believed that Shaler had agreed to the eight-months-and-a-day delay. This Shaler stoutly denied, and concluded not to wait for Chauncey but to inform the Dey that no such delay could be tolerated. There must be an immediate treaty. Finally, the Dey came to terms, but as the next day, Friday, was his Sabbath, Saturday the Sabbath of his interpreter, the Jew Bensamon, and Sunday Shaler's Sabbath, the treaty could not be signed until Monday. During these negotiations the Dey comported himself with dignity and determination, and with no "hasty ebullitions of temper."

Over the week end, Chauncey returned, and Shaler urged him to stay until these protracted negotiations were finished. He did remain a few days, but the return of the fierce storms made it necessary for him once again to take the fleet back to Mahon, leaving only the long-suffering *Spark* in the tempestuous bay. These same tempests delayed the signing which had been set for the 23rd, for a terrible storm on the evening of the 22nd kept the Dey busy supervising the work of saving water-front property. Once again the *Spark* nearly foundered. This strenuous experience gave the Dey an excuse to go to the country for a rest, and it was not until Christmas that the formalities were concluded. That same day Handy boarded the *Spark* to carry the document to Chauncey at Port Mahon, much to the relief of the captain and the crew of that sore-buffeted vessel. This second treaty was to be the law between the two powers for years to come. It had been finally achieved by two naval expeditions and the havoc wrought by the British bombardment. This time the task was finished.

# 7. Diplomat Turned Philosopher

SHALER and the naval commanders had accomplished their mission. Never again would the North African pirates levy blackmail on the United States. The American consul must, however, now face a problem which he was to find more difficult, the problem of existence, sometimes no mean problem for an ambitious self-made man. He began to grasp some of the implications of this challenge by a kind of emotional reaction to success which produced depression. He was tired of the mission and anxious to return home. Just before Exmouth's bombardment he had written, "In the course of years, this dreary place would hardly furnish a single event worth retailing, unless the roasting of Jews and the strangling of Turks be regarded as such." Also there seemed no future in the post, and so far he had been unable to save anything from his salary. He was a poor man, and, since his brother Nathaniel had perished in the War of 1812, his family was dependent upon him. Worst of all, he had lost his feeling of superiority: "I am not qualified for any employment of a higher grade than this is, therefore, this must be the extreme limit of my diplomatic honors." In order to persuade Monroe to release him, he may have been oversanguine about the durability of peace. Wishful thinking may have convinced him that he might advise the State Department, despite Captain Oliver Hazard Perry's dissent, that the fleet might safely be withdrawn. This was counsel of which he was later to repent.

125

With the task at Algiers accomplished, Shaler next turned his attention to his other consular charges, Tunis and Tripoli. Since it would be some time before he could receive an answer to his request for a recall, he planned to visit Thomas D. Anderson and Richard B. Jones, the consuls stationed in these kingdoms. In Tunis, particularly, his presence was needed because of trouble that had arisen over injuries to an American citizen. He set forth determined on a show of authority, "well satisfied that any relaxation of a just and severe discipline in support of our new system [no tribute] towards the Barbary powers will inevitably tend to the injury of our credit and of our interests." He left Algiers on May 8, 1817, leaving his secretary, William Buell, in charge of his office.

At Gibraltar Shaler was delayed by fever, and by a recuperative trip to Italy. His visits to Naples, Messina, and Syracuse caused him to ponder the message "of the crumbling monuments of the greatness of nations whose existence has passed away but the rays of whose glory still shine upon us." It was not until September that he finally reached Tunis and Tripoli in the company of Chauncey who had returned to the Mediterranean. As a result of his tour, Shaler was able to adjust several problems of varying seriousness, including the difficult question of whether the American consul should kiss the foot of the Bey of Tunis. A treaty with that monarch was also concluded. Since Shaler's investigation showed him that there was no natural dependence of the other Barbary consulates upon that of Algiers, he recommended that each be made independent of the Consul General, a recommendation later accepted by Monroe.

Bad news prevented Shaler's return to Algiers. The plague had broken out, and death stalked the streets. This terrifying figure was accompanied by revolution and the overthrow of the Dey. The misfortunes of the Algerine monarch had been too much for him: he had been beaten by the British, he had been forced to sign a second treaty with the United States, and now the plague was scourging his subjects. It was evident that his fanatical people saw him as the object of divine displeasure, so they destroyed him— "the only man," Shaler believed, "amongst them who appeared capable of sustaining their rickety fortunes." A religious fanatic, Ali Khodgia, described by Shaler as an "old imbecile shopkeeper," organized the Turkish Janissaries against Omar, and having killed him with their aid, shut himself up in the fortress and began a high-handed rule.

The first task of the new Dey was to rid himself of the Turkish soldiers and to make his government hereditary. With the assistance of native tribesmen he succeeded in slaughtering a number of the Janissaries. He also sought to make his rule a social success, and gathered about him a harem of beautiful girls. The fact that most of these girls were Jewesses, some of whom enjoyed British citizenship, suggested the desirability of religious zeal for proselyting, and the new Dey began with his Jewish interpreter, whom he insisted should turn Mohammedan. The linguist refused, despite offers of promotion, claiming the protection of British citizenship. Such defiance infuriated the Dey. Immediately he had a fire kindled—he would burn Bensamon at the stake. The sight of the flames caused the interpreter to swoon; when he revived, he found that his head had been shaved and that he was dressed as a Musselman. When the British Consul protested this action, the Dey opened a door and showed the interpreter a number of recently severed heads; he threatened to add his to the collection if he did not acquiesce.

These reports confirmed Shaler in his determination not to return to Algiers until the plague subsided, and he settled himself at Marseilles to direct at long distance the performance of consular duties by Buell. A problem loomed most formidably. The usual semipiratical fleets which put out from Algiers might well carry the plague infection with them, and woe betide any ship which fell in with them. Buell reported that the Dey claimed to be friendly, but Shaler was suspicious, partly because Anderson wrote from Tunis that the Bey had repudiated the September treaty with the United States and had made an alliance with Algiers. That cruisers were being armed foretold piratical forays.

Dr. George Eustis, American Minister to the Hague, was wintering in Marseilles for his health, and both diplomats worked on the problem. After full discussion Shaler sent Buell his instructions. He was to tell the Dey that the President of the United States had been informed that Algerines would not molest American ships. Buell was also to tell him that, because of the plague, it was necessary that the Dey "make an explicit declaration that in future all commanders of Algiers cruisers shall receive his positive instructions not to board any American merchant vessel during the existence of pestilence in his dominions on any pretext whatsoever." He was further to impress upon the Dey that such aggression would be considered "an act of hostility of the most aggravated nature."

Buell reported in due time that he had given the Dey Shaler's demands, to which the Dey had replied that the flag of the United States was often flown by others and that he must board some ships in order to prevent this deception. Could not bona fide American ships display a signal? Shaler instructed Buell to tell him the United States would stoop to no signals and would hold the Dey accountable for any violations.

While these policies were being worked out, Shaler left Marseilles for Sicily in March, 1818, aboard the U.S.S. *Franklin,* the flagship of the newly arrived Commodore Stewart. From there he proceeded to Tunis and then to Algiers, where he found the plague still raging. He did not go ashore at Algiers, but learned that the bloodthirsty Dey had died of the plague, and that a new Dey had been legally elected by the Divan. Power was once again in the hands of the Turks. The new regime seemed more inclined to respect American rights, and the Algerine fleet was kept at home that spring. From Algiers Shaler proceeded to Leghorn, the new rendezvous of the fleet, where he planned to settle down with the satisfied feeling that "it has been my lot in Barbary, at least in Algiers, to substitute a system of political relations upon a footing of independence and economy, in the place of one that was tributary and of unbounded extravagance." For all his satisfaction, however, he was still hoping to be relieved and allowed to go home.

When the cessation of the plague finally permitted Shaler to return to Algiers in the fall of 1819, his responsibilities were relaxed. He had accomplished his mission, insofar as he had made the name of the United States respected on the shores of Barbary. He sought from time to time to be transferred to other duties, but the State Department kept him at his post—none knew better than he how to handle this peculiar people. Save for a leave during the winter of 1821–1822, which he spent in the United States, Shaler was to remain on the shores of the Mediterranean for nine more years. He did not complain too much. Not only was great consideration shown him, both public and private, but some of his driving ambition was flagging with the advance of years. Furthermore, he could now save $1,000 or more a year, and was prospering. He even admitted he was beginning to set a higher value upon the luxuries of fine climate, abundance, and leisure. It was up to the State Department, he felt, to dispose of him. "I am growing fat, I am becoming a water drinker. I have become a moderate reasonable politician but what will surprise you the most I am a poet, and as far as I have gone, no very mean one."

Shaler had really grown quite contented in Algiers, which had become known to Americans in the Mediterranean as the "Old Consul's Bay." Here he kept watch, and grew in his understanding of its strange people. As he wrote Bainbridge: "The Algerines, though a sensible people, pay no attention to abstract arguments; they reason only upon experience and palpable facts. . . . These Barbarians are generally cunning and cowardly but capable of an activity that is really admirable, it is my opinion that they can equip a fleet for sea with more dispatch than any other people. . . . Morocco is null as a marauding power, and in Tunis and Tripoli we have a certain guaranty for good conduct in the hereditary form of these governments. But the Government of Algiers is always that of a predominant faction liable every day to be overturned, the present only is important to them, as they openly prefer to rely alone upon pyracy for existence being without agriculture, commerce or arts . . . the standing that we have acquired here is irksome and vexatious to all the governments of Europe, to some because they wish not, and to others because they cannot follow our example. . . . I have endeavored to make them comprehend that we have nothing in view beyond the maintenance of the positive security of our flag and the respect which is due our character in Barbary."

These years, however, were not without incident. Twice

Shaler was called upon to participate in delicate negotiations. In 1822, when he returned from his American sojourn, he found his position in danger. He had left his nephew and namesake, William Shaler, in charge of the consulate when he departed for home, but the youth was irresponsible and prone to escapades. From Commodore Jones his uncle received an unpleasant report. William, it seems, had gone into the country one day on a hunting expedition without "that attendance proper to denote his quality and procure for him the desired security when he quitted the highway," which he had so often been warned to take. He followed an accustomed path and was surprised to be halted by an armed guard. The construction of a canal had recently been undertaken by the Algerine Ministry of War, and a guard had been stationed to keep strangers away from the new work. When young Shaler defied the guard and threatened him with his gun, the young man was tumbled from his horse in the very presence of the war minister himself.

Enraged and humiliated, the young man had tried unsuccessfully to make a diplomatic incident of it; the Dey would not take him seriously. He had already had difficulty with Buell because of the "lightness and irregularity of his conduct," and young Shaler seemed just as irresponsible. The Algerine sovereign sought a meeting of the other consuls to discuss the question. They refused to become involved, and the Dey dropped the matter until the elder Shaler returned. This attitude so aroused William, Jr., that he left the country to await his uncle at Port Mahon. When the Consul first heard the story, he thought the attack might be premeditated. He soon changed his mind, and sent his nephew home to the United States. Reaching Algiers on November 16, 1822, three months after the incident, he learned that the Dey was inclined to forget the matter. But not Shaler. White men, and particularly citizens of the United States, could not afford to lose face with these natives. Taking a firm stand, Shaler told the Dey "that the outrage which had been offered to the Government of the United States" in the presence of one of his principal ministers "was of a character too serious for me to decide upon inasmuch as it involved peace or war," and he had therefore referred the matter to Washington. He knew that his position was tenuous, but he had to uphold his nephew. Withdrawing to his consulate, Shaler held no further communication with the Dey. This was all he could do, for when he finally heard from John Quincy Adams, he learned that the Secretary considered it only a petty insult for which the youth was in large part responsible, and that it must be noticed no further.

Shaler was, perforce, brought out of his retirement the next year by a new rampage of the Algerine Dey. These were the times of the Greek rebellion against Turkish misrule, and so strong had been the Greek spirit that the Porte had called upon its Barbary vassals for aid. The Dey of Algiers had entered the conflict with some degree of success and had been stimulated thereby to return to piracy. In October, 1823, he decided to begin depredations on European and American commerce and to resume Christian slavery. He believed he could now defy the powers with safety and sought an opportunity to test his strength.

The occasion for this defiance was an outbreak on the Algerian frontier among the Kabyles, an independent group of tribes which had never been controlled by the Turkish rulers of Algeria. In the course of the hostilities a Turkish official had been carried into the mountains as a hostage. The Dey, seeking reprisal, turned upon the consuls of the Powers, because a number of Kabyles were servants in Algiers, particularly in the consular households. Condemning these tribesmen to death, the Dey attempted to arrest them. He made demands upon the various consuls for the surrender of their servants, and most of the consulates complied. McDonnell and Shaler refused. Shaler had two of these young men in his household and had no intention of turning them over to probable death. His house was respected, but that of the British Consul, who was unpopular, was violated and the servants dragged out. McDonnell was anxious that all the consuls join in signing a remonstrance against this action of the Dey. At first Shaler was not willing to comply, because he felt that the other consuls had not co-operated but had weakly surrendered their rights. At length, however, he consented, when he was permitted to draft the remonstrance based upon the general principles of international usage.

During this dispute, the Algerines were preparing for war with Spain. Early in January, 1824, prizes began to be brought into Algiers, their crews quite apparently being enslaved. When the British Consul protested, the Dey declared that the treaty made by Exmouth had expired and that Christian slavery had begun anew. Hardly had this defiance been uttered when a British frigate appeared with orders for the Dey to sign new articles to be added to former treaties. The Algerines were to agree never again to violate a consulate, and to permit the British flag to fly from the consulate in the town. The Dey refused to sign, and on January 29th McDonnell and his family withdrew to the frigate. Although some concessions were made by the Dey, he would not agree to permit the flag to fly in the city of Algiers. The frigate sailed off with the McDonnells, leaving British interests in the charge of Shaler. That day, January 31st, the British fired on an Algerine war vessel off Algiers, and the

Algerines declared a state of war. Shaler then turned his efforts toward persuading the Dey of the folly of war with England, and even undertook to send a letter from the Dey to the English government through the American minister in London.

On February 22nd a British fleet appeared in Algiers under command of Vice-Admiral Sir Harry B. Neale, accompanied by McDonnell. Shaler went aboard the flagship to tender his good offices and to report that the British consulate was undisturbed and that McDonnell's agent was carrying on his affairs. The admiral, in turn, informed Shaler that he was to blockade the port until the Dey signed the additional articles and made amends to the Consul.

After a day of sickness, for Shaler was beginning to suffer from attacks of sick headache which were to occur with increasing frequency, he tried to persuade the Dey to see reason in the affair. This was not easy, for the Dey himself was in a difficult position. It would violate a deep-seated religious prejudice to allow the British flag to fly inside the walls of Algiers. The populace was fanatical about it, and he would raise a storm of protest if he yielded on this point, particularly to McDonnell. The citizens still held the British Consul responsible for Exmouth's bombardment, and the Dey knew that he was dangerous to him as long as he remained. He therefore welcomed this opportunity to refuse to allow McDonnell to return.

Shaler kept up his efforts for a month, encouraged by the desires of most of the Algerine officials to avoid war, but he found the Dey "impractical" and fatalistic. All he gained was the ill-will of the potentate. After a month of blockading, the Vice-Admiral pressed for an answer, and at length went ashore on March 28th for an interview in which the Dey again refused to yield. The admiral threatened to leave if McDonnell were not received, but the Dey refused to make any decision until he had heard directly from the British government in answer to his letter. The blockade continued.

After three more months of blockading British patience was exhausted, and by July 11th a large fleet had assembled and made preparation for bombardment. Some skirmishes occurred and occasional shots were fired until the 25th, when an agreement was finally reached. The British retreated from their stand by not pressing the flag privilege and by agreeing, on motives of humanity, not to insist on McDonnell's return for fear of his being killed. The Algerines in their turn signed the articles, again agreed to renounce Christian slavery and to receive a British Proconsul, Danford.

Shaler was disgusted at this outcome because he was attached to McDonnell and his family and thought that the British should have insisted on their return. However, he received Danford into his home and set about advising him on his consular duties. Shaler noted with pride that his own standing with the Algerines had not suffered; he was well satisfied with himself, a fact he did not hide in his dispatches to Washington.

These later years were not wholly concerned with diplomacy, for Shaler was returning to an old interest. Scholarly pursuits had always attracted him, and he was tempted in the leisure of his consulate to return to this enticing pastime. Just before he had terminated his furlough in 1822, an eminent scholar had sought him out. Peter S. Duponceau, noted Philadelphia lawyer and officer of the American Philosophical Society, had begun a correspondence with Shaler regarding the languages of northern Africa. He was particularly interested in the speech of those tribes descended from the pre-Mohammedan peoples who had flourished before the conquest. No one knew much of the Berber dialects, and Duponceau asked Shaler to gather information regarding them and to supply vocabulary lists. This task appealed to Shaler's scholarly bent and he now went to work on it. In due time, he sent several reports to Duponceau which were discussed in the American Philosophical Society and published by them.

These reports to Duponceau aroused his interest in philology in general. Feeling that he needed more knowledge as background for his Berber studies, he studied Greek and Latin. To his old friend Senator Johnston of Louisiana he wrote: "You doubtless recollect that I stupidly refused to join you in the study of the Latin when I was last in Washington on the pretext of its being too late? Well, I have since become a most devoted classical student, and I have really overcome all the great obstacles in the way of my being rather a good scholar. As I provided myself with elementary books in France I had occasion to remark the excellency of their methods for studying the classical languages. They appear to me superior to ours in simplicity of arrangement and perspicuity of demonstration. My Greek grammar was composed in 1813 by an illustrious professor for the use of the celebrated normal school in France . . . ; it has gone through the 13th edition and is the best synopsis of any language that I have ever seen. It entered into my plan of study to make a complete translation of this grammar and finding as I proceeded that I could do it justice, I have determined to make a fair and correct copy of it in order for publication, if it should be judged sufficiently useful by my literary friends at home." Unfortunately, he was to learn that someone else had published such a translation in Baltimore.

In this work he was aided by the arrival of a competent secretary, William B. Hodgson, who joined him in the spring of 1826. Shaler had urged for some time that he be sent a scholarly assistant, part of whose duties would be the investigation of North African dialects. At one time he had even thought of bringing over a child who would be brought up to speak them, and had written to Duponceau about it. But none could be found. He had then considered having one of his younger nephews try it. Now, however, a young man of scholarly tastes had been selected, and undertook these philological studies upon his arrival. Shaler found him apt, and when the Consul left Barbary in 1828, Hodgson continued reporting to the American Philosophical Society on North African languages. These two diplomats had thus extended the bounds of knowledge as well as the interests of the young republic.

Shaler's scholarly interests were not circumscribed by the bounds of philology. He aspired to write for a wider audience. From the very beginning of his sojourn in Barbary, he had been curious about these people and their customs. He had collected a mass of information regarding Algiers, its people, their environment and their behavior. These data he worked into a narrative which had a double purpose—to give information and to promote an idea.

His experiences had demonstrated the necessity of destroying these pirates. The Powers, or one of them at least, should wipe out this nest which threatened Christian interests. Shaler was anxious to do what he could to spread the idea of the conquest of Barbary. He had viewed the terrain of Algiers on various excursions into the country, and he had studied the military plans used by former conquerors. He reviewed his findings at length in his book. He explained that previous expeditions had made their attacks the hard way, by landing in the bay east of Algiers. Instead, the attacking force should approach from the west. Ten miles to the west of the city was the bay of Sidi Ferrajh. The road from this bay to Algiers could be covered on horseback in three hours, and there were copious springs of water along the way. The only fortification in that direction was a "castle" about a mile from the Casauba in Algiers, so situated that it might be commanded from heights. Shaler believed this could be "scaled and breached by a mine in a short time." There batteries might be planted on heights commanding the citadel itself. While this was being accomplished, the fleet which had brought the land force would sail to Algiers and enter the bay stripped for action.

Shaler supplied with these general strategical directions minute information regarding the fortifications and the strength of the garrisons. From these details he turned to general policy. He was still thinking in terms of his memorandum written in 1812, in which he had proposed to divide much of the world between the United States and England. He now argued at length that "it would be for the general interests of the world that Great Britain should determine to occupy and colonize this portion of Africa."

Jared Sparks, a friend of Cleveland's, had recently become editor of the *North American Review* and had asked Shaler for some articles on Algiers. Shaler now looked to him to arrange for the publication of his book. He was anxious that it should appear in print, for he had received no commendation from the State Department for his work as peacemaker during the recent British expedition. He therefore hastily added an account of his part in the difficulties which were brought to a climax in November, 1824. Despite his interest in British advance in North Africa, or perhaps because of it, he belabored the conduct of that armada. He emphasized his own resourcefulness and the "tameness" of the "preposterous expedition" which had ended in realizing the fable of the mountain in labor, "despite the fact that it numbered twenty-three sail" sufficient to "raze Algiers to its foundations." This manuscript he sent off in March, 1825.

Shaler's *Sketches of Algiers* appeared during the next year and attracted a certain amount of attention. The commander of the British expedition, Sir Harry Neale, took quick umbrage, and immediately set about to answer it. In a pamphlet with the formidable title, "A Reply to Erroneous Statements and Unwarranted Reflections in a Publication entitled 'Sketches of Algiers' by William Shaler," the British Admiral stated flatly that all Shaler had done was to come aboard his ship upon the arrival of the fleet and communicate the Dey's pacific intentions. He contradicted a number of Shaler's claims, and charged that he could have gotten most of his information only from Bensamon, whose understanding of English was imperfect. On the whole, the criticisms were not serious, and we are led to believe that Neale was more exasperated at Shaler's general contempt for the British, or as Neale put it, "the illiberality of sentiment pervading the censure which I have been called upon to repel." Shaler's reply to this has not survived—Sparks would not accept it for publication. It is to be noted that the British made no effort to follow Shaler's suggestions by invading North Africa in the region of Algiers.

Shaler and his book were to have more influence with the French. He spent the summer of 1825, before his work appeared, renewing old acquaintances in France. There he suggested to such influential men as Hyde de Neuville that

French enterprise should encompass Algiers. No action was taken immediately, but his words were not forgotten, and when his book appeared it had some French circulation and was printed in a French translation. Events were shaping the policy of France along the lines Shaler had suggested.

Trouble between Algiers and the French was brewing. Shaler had become ill of gallstones and dropsy in the fall of 1826, and by spring was so sick that his life was despaired of. He was taken to Spanish mineral baths where he spent most of 1827 in slow recuperation. During his absence the Dey of Algiers had become incensed at the French. The latter had a concession for coral fishing on the coast of Algeria and had erected a bastion there to protect the industry. The French now undertook to enlarge this fortification without the consent of the Dey. He complained to the French ministry, and felt insulted when the Consul told him that his protests must be made only through the Consul and not directly to the French government. The potentate in his rage struck the Consul and so precipitated a crisis. In June, 1827, the French began a blockade of the port of Algiers which they were maintaining in some half-hearted fashion when Shaler returned in October.

It was plain to Shaler that the French policy was not effective. He himself was winding up his affairs preparatory to returning home. His prolonged illness had warned him that he could stay in Algeria no longer, so he had once more applied for his recall. In February, 1828, the good news arrived. He was further gratified to learn that his scholarly efforts had been crowned by election to the American Philosophical Society. He now hoped to go back to Latin America, having been promised the Havana consulate whenever Spain might allow the establishment of an agent of the

United States in that port. The diplomatic grapevine bore rumors that such an opportunity was about due. William Shaler left Algiers on April 3, 1828, nearly thirteen years after he first sighted it, directing his route homeward through France.

Once more he took the opportunity to urge France to take over Algeria. He reported to those in authority on the unsatisfactory state of the blockade and pressed for more decisive action. The French government was not yet ready, but a decision was not far off. Finally, in 1830, the die was cast. In January the council of state adopted a plan presented by a young naval officer, Abel Aubert Dupetit-Thouars, for the invasion of Algeria. He was, interestingly enough, a relative of the famous botanist, Louis Marie-Aubert Dupetit-Thouars, whom Shaler probably had met nearly thirty years before on the Isle of France. Dupetit-Thouars' plan was very similar to that of Shaler, and the French expedition which captured Algeria in July, 1830, followed the general strategy laid down by the American consul.

There is little, if any, reason to believe that in mapping out the invasion of Algeria in 1942 the Anglo-American board of strategy studied Shaler's plans, but it is of more than passing interest to note that on November 8, 1942, the American shock troops landed at Sidi Ferrajh and proceeded against Algiers just as Shaler advised in 1826.

This advance agent of American interests on the shores of Barbary had reflected some of the unusual characteristics of the epoch. His imagination and his self-developed talents had enabled him to transcend the trammels of routine duty at a far-off consulate and to make a real contribution to the world of learning. This diplomat turned philosopher created a monument for himself of a character which entitles him to a not unhonored place in the ranks of those who shared the spectacular genius of that age of reason so superbly illustrated on the grand scale by Franklin and Jefferson.

# 8. The Pearl of the Antilles

FOR fifty years the United States had sought to gain free access to the ports of Cuba. For fifty years agents of all temperaments and ambitions had sought to further the interests of the republic. Seldom had success attended their efforts but the hope persisted and now Shaler believed that he might at length succeed. Since his first attempt in 1810 various others had followed in his footsteps with little better success. Madison, Monroe, John Quincy Adams and Henry Clay had all been concerned over the fate of Cuba. The Pearl of the Antilles lay at the gateway of the nation, dominating important approaches to the United States, and its trade was a rich prize. Possession of either the island or its commerce by any power save Spain could not be tolerated. Therefore every sign of revolt, every suspicion of design for capture by other powers was jealously watched and the hope that Cuba might someday cast her lot with the United States continued to be cherished.

Two years after Shaler's first visit, Spain had adopted her liberal constitution of 1812 and this brave act caused Madison to imagine that Spain under the new regime might let down the bars to trade and consuls while fighting Napoleon. No agents had been there since the departure of Shaler and Rogers, save Richard M. Bell commissioned by Rogers as vice consul at Santiago and Vincent Gray still resident in Havana and available for occasional clandestine service. So Stephen Kingston and John Mitchell of Pennsylvania were sent to Havana and Santiago. Not only were they to render regular services as commercial agents but they were to watch for signs of any attempt by a foreign power to seize Cuba and also to encourage the idea of annexation to the United States. Madison and Monroe shared the dreads and dreams of Jefferson.

Neither of these agents was recognized and both were soon sent home. But Kingston was there long enough to discover a spark of the love of liberty under the mass of Spanish governmental corruption. The Spanish officials, however, suspected that he like Shaler might be an active agent in blowing this spark up into a flame. Gray and Bell again were left to do what they could to represent the United States in Cuba.

During the War of 1812 there was no further opportunity for such efforts but no sooner was that conflict over than Monroe renewed his efforts. He had a valid excuse, for Spain held Americans captured in Florida in the recent conflict. Also piracy was flagrant. The Revolutionists were still active in most of the Spanish colonies and republican governments were fighting for existence. Under these new flags various freebooters sailed the Spanish Main seeking prizes. Though there was no revolution in Cuba, various local captains indulged in this nefarious practice and even citizens of the United States were not above such ventures. England and the United States sent war vessels which on occasion battled with the pirates. Monroe despatched two representatives, Eligius Fromentine and James Brown, to seek the release of the prisoners only to receive them back empty-handed.

Changing economic conditions focused attention upon another endeavor to establish a commercial agent. In 1817 Spain abolished the tobacco monopoly in Cuba and the next year opened her ports to world commerce. These acts stimulated a vigorous trade. Also important political conditions made the United States anxious for close watch and accurate news. England had persuaded Spain to abolish the slave trade and was proceeding to aid her in enforcing the prohibition. The State Department feared that Great Britain might use this as an excuse to take over the island or to spread abolition propaganda in the southern United States.

In view of these new developments Monroe and John Quincy Adams commissioned George P. Stevenson of Baltimore, December 13, 1817, to make another attempt. He moved quietly and was permitted to remain without a sign of official recognition. Occasionally he exercised some of the functions of an agent but it was barren labor and within a year he returned, leaving his slight duties to Vincent Gray. This convenient citizen had married a Louisiana creole, had formed a partnership with a Cuban and had been given the rights of a Spaniard regarding commerce. He could carry on very well between agents.

Trade grew. During 1818–1819 from fifty to sixty United States ships came to Cuban ports each month. Also the difficulties over Florida were cleared up when Spain ceded that province to her neighbor to the north. Encouraged by this success Monroe and Adams sent another agent, Michael Hogan, to try his luck at Havana. When he arrived, Cuba was practically independent. The revolution of 1820 in Spain had destroyed what little power of concentration Madrid could muster on her remaining colony and left the island to its own devices. What could she do?

Piracy increased and this brought an enlarged British squadron. The Irish eyes of Hogan saw "Conquest" written on its sails. The French, too, were to be feared. Furthermore the new revolutionary governments in Mexico and

Colombia were on the verge of success. Might not Cuba be moved to follow their example and strike for independence?

These conditions dictated keeping an agent constantly on the alert. Therefore, when Hogan was sent on to Valparaiso in 1821, his place was immediately filled by John Warner of Wilmington, friend of Senator Caesar A. Rodney of Delaware. He shared the apprehension of Hogan and Gray regarding British and French designs and though unrecognized he likewise participated in the commercial prosperity of the island. In 1822, 669 United States merchantmen entered Havana and 200 came into Matagorda. Warner was an ardent annexationist, like his patron Rodney, and he sought to make connections with Cuban patriots. He went into business with a Cuban of like mind, José del Castillo, who had been educated in Baltimore. His efforts aroused the suspicions of the Captain-General and his official acts provoked the hostility of the local notaries whose fees were thereby diminished. His agency was closed, but this was Cuba and despite this edict Warner continued to function until 1825. He kept his friend Rodney informed about the prospects of annexation and the political annexations in the United States.

At no time during Warner's term was Washington easy about Cuba. Piracy continued to flourish and the Navy Department in 1822 gave one of its captains, James Biddle, diplomatic powers to negotiate with the Captain-General for permission to pursue these pirates into Cuban territory. He and his successor, David Porter, were very vigorous in this regard, but met little success as diplomats. At the same time, piratical forays from Puerto Rico were so bad that when Joel R. Poinsett was despatched southward as the first American envoy to Mexico in September 1822, he was directed to stop at that island and protest to the authorities.

They in turn feared that filibusters from the United States had designs on Puerto Rico.

The possibility of French or British annexation was always disturbing and Monroe and his cabinet spent much time in studying Cuban policy. In 1822 a Cuban agent, Bernabé Sánchez, sought help in Washington for a revolution which would liberate Cuba and bring its people into the American Union. No help was granted him but watchful eyes were constantly on the alert. More disturbing was the report of Minister Gallatin from Paris in the spring of 1823 that Spain might cede Cuba to Great Britain in return for help against France, then about to invade Spain to restore Ferdinand VII. This brought from Washington notice to Spain that the United States would not tolerate any cession and would regard any effort on Spain's part to transfer Cuba as justification for Cuban revolt and aid by the United States to this effort. Once more the United States demanded the recognition of its consuls.

The appearance of a French frigate off Havana in July, 1823, caused a flurry. The Cuban authorities feared that it was a forerunner to invasion and refused to permit it to enter. Gray, who was momentarily pinch-hitting for Warner, urged that the United States send a fleet to these waters "as it might, in case of a change of affairs, greatly tend to attach this country to the United States on the score of friendship and commerce." None of the dreaded events occurred, French and British vessels came and went without changing the island's status. The Captain-General put down certain weak efforts at revolt and when Warner left finally in 1825 all was relatively quiet.

This calm was short-lived, as Warner's successor found. The Adams-Clay administration appointed T. M. Rodney of the famous Delaware family to succeed Warner. He had enjoyed a brief experience as assistant to Warner and his political connections caused him to be elevated despite the hopes of the long-accommodating Gray that he might have the post. The appearance of a French fleet in Cuban waters and an invitation extended by Colombia for a general congress of American republics at Panama again aroused apprehensions. The French fleet might seize Cuba. The Panama Congress might authorize Colombia or Mexico to aid Cuba in revolt and thus pave the way for European intervention. Clay restated the Monroe Doctrine as a warning to France or Great Britain and despatched Daniel Pope Cook of Illinois to discuss with Cuban authorities the defense of the island. He was probably to assure them of protection and perhaps to feel out the possibility of annexation. But he was taken ill on the journey and returned shortly. The record of his achievement if any is blank.

Most disturbing to Rodney was the decline in trade which this uncertainty and continuing piracy produced. As Rodney's fees declined his reports reflected a pessimism natural in the circumstances. Though the pirates were being more effectively suppressed by an augmented Spanish fleet, the restored Bourbons were aiming heavy blows at the shipping of the United States, carrying three-quarters of the Cuban trade. Ferdinand VII was returning to the mercantilism interrupted by the chaos in Spanish government inaugurated by Napoleon. New interpretations of the age-old tonnage duties were published and specific levies increased. American vessels were compelled to pay two dollars and a half a ton, though Spanish shipping paid one-fifth of that sum in the ports of the United States. Flour from Spain in a Spanish vessel was taxed fifty cents a barrel but foreign flour in foreign bottoms was assessed fifteen times that sum. Indignant at such discrimination, Adams and Clay instructed their Spanish minister, Alexander H. Everett, to demand a reduction of such tribute and once again to seek the right to send a regular consul to Havana. Everett's efforts in the latter cause seemed to show some signs of success and Shaler was encouraged to believe as he left Algiers that such might be the fact. Would Monroe's promise that he would be the first consul be redeemed?

Shaler arrived home on the eve of the Jacksonian triumph. A new regime was on its way to Washington and among its members were good friends of the Algerine Consul. Martin Van Buren was to be Secretary of State and Shaler's long-standing Clinton-Van Buren connections would be influential. His old friend, Edward Livingston, was a Louisiana Senator and Jonathan Russell was now a Jacksonian Democrat. Shortly after Jackson was inaugurated his case was considered. Rodney of course was through, he was not of the elect and Jackson had no difficulty in agreeing upon Shaler. He resigned his Algerine post, April 8, 1829, on the promise of the Havana consulate, and five days later a dispatch was received from Everett that Spain had agreed to permit a consul to be received at Havana. As it would take some time to make the necessary arrangements with Spain, Shaler was to have the summer to settle his affairs.

He was commissioned September 8, 1829 and late in October he set forth with a considerable retinue. His friend Cleveland had suffered in fortune and now Shaler could befriend him. He and his wife were to accompany the consul-designate as vice-consul and housekeeper respectively. A nephew, John Truly Shaler, William's younger brother, was to be the consul's secretary. But the anticipated triumphal entry was marred by an unpleasant surprise. The slow-moving Spanish government had forwarded no exequatur and without it, the Captain-General, though cordial, would not grant official recognition. Shaler, therefore, like his predecessors must function unofficially until such time as the document should arrive.

The Havana in which he must settle down and wait had not changed much since he left it in 1811. It was still unpaved, still the city of narrow streets and heavy fortifications, still dirty, still scourged by plagues. It was a difficult and expensive place in which to live. Suitable houses were scarce and rents high and he and his household had to establish themselves in a dwelling with decided drawbacks. It was more than usually hot in summer, it had no carriage house and its rent was $1,020 per annum. The servant problem made life even more complicated and he had to pay a Negro man and woman $480 a year. The receipts of his office were to be in the neighborhood of $6,500 annually and as he paid Cleveland $2,000 he was to find the office much less lucrative than he had hoped.

The people of Havana were much as they had been before. The local planters were still inclined to be friendly with the United States, even though the government was not. There were still many grievances against greedy Spanish officials. Some whom Shaler had known on his first visit were still active and one of them immediately sought him out. Don Francisco Arango was now sixty-five years old but still the power among the planters and in the Royal Consulado. He discussed at length with Shaler the unsatisfactory commercial situation. The revived mercantilism of Spain was driving foreign vessels and goods away from Cuban ports and markets. Also Spain was trying to revive the custom of granting monopolies to Spanish favorites. The colonists therefore were forced to pay Spanish prices unmodified by much foreign competition.

The planting interests, Arango reported, had hoped in

vain that the United States could cause Spain to enter a tariff agreement; now they were considering an alternative. The Royal Consulado wished to propose to Spain that it be permitted to make an agreement with the United States directly on such matters. Before presenting such a proposal to the Spanish authorities Arango desired to arrive at an informal understanding with the United States government. He protested against the United States tariff and intimated that if the United States would again admit Cuban molasses, duties on flour and tonnage from the northern republic might be reciprocally lowered.

Shaler was greatly interested and reported to his government, meanwhile pointing out in his turn to Arango the iniquities of the Spanish regulations. Nothing came of his report, however. Van Buren had already renewed protests to Spain against the high duties but he was not ready for any informal understandings with local colonial authorities. Shaler could only wait, watch and deplore the facts of his situation. It was exasperating to know that 1,200 ships entered and cleared the island from or to the United States annually. Yet though Great Britain, France, Holland and Prussia all had representatives at Havana in full standing, the United States must be content with a "tolerated notary," as Shaler described himself. But the long delay was soon to end. When Shaler came back from a leave of absence during which he had barely survived shipwreck on his return voyage, he found the exequatur finally at hand. In January, 1831, he could report that he was recognized. After fifty years of effort the United States had established a consul in Havana. Shaler was the first citizen of the United States to enjoy such a distinction.

His recognition brought him little opportunity to render the service he always desired to give to his government. At first only petty difficulties seemed to come before him, waterfront rows and stranded sailors, complaints against pirates and the settlement of the estates of invalids who came to Cuba to get well and more frequently died. In 1832, the specter of British designs upon the island again aroused apprehension. England abolished slavery in the British West Indian possessions, an act prompted according to Shaler's uncharitable judgment, partly by a desire to ruin the prosperity of Cuba and to excite discord and servile war in the southern United States. He feared it would precipitate such chaos in Cuba that the United States would be forced to intervene. The creoles, he reported, would welcome such intervention. He had reason to believe that he might this time be more effective.

Van Buren had retired from the State Department and his place had been taken during the previous year by an old friend of Shaler's, Edward Livingston of Louisiana. When word of England's action was reported, Livingston expressed immediate interest and at his request Shaler not only sent copies of his former dispatches and reports but also when he visited the United States during the summer of 1832 he conferred with his chief. The burden of his thought was the same as it had been twenty years before.

The creoles resented the exactions of Spanish officials but their resentment was unorganized. He felt sure, however, that they were more friendly to the United States than during his former visit; no longer did he hear the ill-natured and contemptuous remarks against his country that he had formerly had to swallow. If they were sure that the United States would help them, their fear of a slave revolt might be capitalized. Besides, that country could not afford to let the latter catastrophe materialize so near to the Southern States. He sent a lengthy list of creoles who might be counted on and described each of them. He recommended frequent calls from war vessels of the United States and the establishment of postal relations to make communication easier.

Through all his writing and talking there appeared his very apparent desire to be authorized to convey to the Cuban creoles in a most discreet fashion the sympathy of the United States government toward their hopes. He was confident that if he were entrusted with the conciliation of Cuban friendship that "the Island of Cuba would become impregnable to any rival power; and that on the first crisis there, it might, if deemed expedient, be as naturally incorporated into this confederation as Louisiana has been."

Livingston never committed himself in writing very definitely to Shaler's plan. He assured him that "at whatever risk that Island must be prevented from passing into any other hands than our own. . . . The great objects of our government in relation to Cuba, are a free and untrammeled trade [and] . . . to preserve it in the hands of Spain, even at the expense of war, and only in the event of finding that impossible to look to its annexation to our confederacy." The annexation of Cuba was bound to raise formidable opposition. The island would be slave territory and the circulation of the *Liberator* was foretelling the great growth of antislavery sentiment in the United States. Livingston realized the dangers and was going to take no immediate step. He urged Shaler to return as quickly as possible to the island and establish a system of frequent correspondence with the other American consuls and commercial agents in Cuba. What the Secretary may have said to Shaler in private conference unfortunately is lost. It is doubtful whether Livingston authorized him to speak to his creole friends on these subjects as he wished "from authority."

Before his return to Havana Livingston placed in his

charge an exceedingly troublesome problem. When Spain surrendered Florida, her officers had taken the archives back to Cuba. As these documents included the land office records, this act in violation of the treaty was most embarrassing. The land commission set up by the United States in Florida to confirm all titles frequently found itself in need of these records for vital information. Since 1821 a series of agents sent to secure these papers armed with royal orders had failed. Excuses had always been found for no action, usually fortified by denials of the existence of the particular files desired.

This delay had invited efforts to push doubtful claims on evidence which lacked confirmation and might have been manufactured. One of the most famous was a grant of large proportions alleged to have been made by some Indians to John Forbes, a claim now pressed by Colin Mitchell, a British merchant in Havana. The United States had contested this title step by step and it was now in the Supreme Court. The federal attorneys were extremely anxious for the official files, particularly the land surveys which they hoped would prove the case invalid. When Jackson became President things moved faster. General Richard K. Call of Florida was sent to Havana in 1829 and his energy and shrewdness enabled him to ascertain definitely that land records did exist in Havana. Acting upon his information Van Buren again sought a royal order for the delivery of these papers. This had at length arrived and in May, 1832, Livingston had dispatched Jeremy Robinson to get the papers. He had arrived while Shaler was in the United States and had undertaken to work through Cleveland.

Robinson had found delay endless. Mitchell quite apparently was interested in preventing these papers from being turned over. He was well entrenched in Havana, for the governor's interpreter, Luis Payne, was his man, so it was charged, and in a position to delay. When Livingston heard of the continued failure of Robinson and Cleveland he instructed Shaler to undertake the matter on his return. The consul got to work in December, 1832, with his characteristic energy. Upon his return Robinson and Cleveland were meeting with an official commission of whom Payne was one, who were examining a few papers and wrangling over procedure. Mitchell was in the background with complete access to the papers, beautifully situated to instruct. Shaler and Robinson were looking for the reports of Pintado, the official surveyor. Not only did they seek these documents in the archives but they began negotiations with Pintado's widow who had many documents which might be revealing. After three months of finesse and procrastination Shaler's persistence and effective procedure, combined probably with the Captain-General's interest in not antagonizing the United States further, brought the affair to a conclusion. On March 8th, Shaler was informed that the papers would be turned over. Eight days later he and Robinson began to examine them and worked daily for nearly a fortnight without finding any confirmation of the Forbes-Mitchell claim.

During these days of his latest triumph, the plague had begun to rage. On March 11th, twenty-three vessels had fled the port. The next day there were 700 dead. Processions marched the streets carrying sacred images. Tar, pitch, brimstone and frankincense were burned in the streets to purify the air. All the ordinance in the fortifications was discharged in the hope that the detonation might dislodge the cholera. People were dying at the rate of 400 a day and within three weeks 3,000 persons had perished. Shaler was all undaunted by these distressing scenes; he had lived through many plagues. Besides, he was used to sickness;

the periodic attacks which had begun in Barbary continued and he had to go to bed with migraine headaches every ten days. On the afternoon of March 27th after a busy day at the Intendancy poring over land surveys, Robinson and Shaler parted. Two hours later, at five in the afternoon, the consul became violently ill with all the distressing symptoms of cholera. Cleveland and his nephew watched all night applying such ineffective remedies as were at hand, but by five in the morning Shaler felt the approach of death. He gave Cleveland his last directions and then in characteristic fashion dismissed him. His great pride asserted itself. No one should see him die. He bade the watchers leave the room and get some rest, he needed them no longer. Left to himself he stretched out to his great length on his back and folded his arms. When the watchers returned two hours later he lay there in that calm relaxation, dead. There was no need for attendants to lay him out for burial, he had done it himself.

Thus ended the career of one of the most active of the advance agents of the United States. He had been in the vanguard in many far places. Whether it was South America, Asia or Africa, in the Atlantic or in the Pacific, in the China Sea or in the Indian Ocean, he had been among the very first to seek advantages for the new republic and spread the gospel of its newly forged liberties.

# 9. The Isles of the Ocean

AS IN Latin America and on the Barbary Coast, American interests in the Pacific were inaugurated and advanced by men who have remained obscure. The first definite commitments to noncontiguous territorial responsibilities in the great Atlantic and Pacific Oceans came to the United States in curious fashion, in the form of claims to dreary atolls scarce visible above the watery wastes of the ocean, coral reefs irregular in shape, sometimes several miles in circumference, devoid of human habitation, where for uncounted centuries myriads of birds had found a resting place.

These islands attracted American interest in the 1840's because farm land, particularly in the upper South, was losing its fertility. Fertilizer was needed and experiments were tried with the bird deposits, or guano, found in great quantity on these scattered isles. The properties of these deposits on islands off the coast of South America had been known to the Incas and in the 1830's, European agriculture had been relearning their use. Notices of such experiments began to be frequent in American agricultural journals in 1842 and 1843 when guano was advertised for sale.

At first, the principal source was the Chincha Islands off the coast of Peru and the government of that country, in return for loans, granted an English firm the concession of selling the guano throughout the world on a commission basis for the benefit of the Peruvian government. The agent of this English company, Gibbs and Company, was Samuel

K. George, a Baltimore dry-goods merchant, who began to sell in 1844 in that city and similar agents took contracts in other large cities. Gibbs and Company controlled the price and kept it high, about forty-seven dollars a ton. Still more aggravating was the fact that the supply was irregular and often inadequate; even if a farmer could pay the price, he was never sure he could get what he needed. But as guano could be purchased only through agents of the English firm, American farmers had to put up with these conditions if they wished the fertilizer. After several years of such unsatisfactory arrangements, agricultural organizations began to urge the State Department to invoke diplomacy to secure more favorable terms from Peru. Their efforts were seconded by other interested parties.

The relations between the United States and Peru at that time were highly unsatisfactory. A treaty of peace, commerce and friendship had been made in 1848 but Peru showed no signs of ratifying it. Furthermore, although Peru had agreed to pay certain claims for damages suffered in her revolution, the installments due under the treaty of 1841 had been paid, neither regularly nor fully, in spite of the vigorous efforts of American diplomacy. The American claimants to whom the money was due became impatient and in 1849 guano was brought into the situation by a petition of a group of the claimants addressed to John M. Clayton, then Secretary of State.

The agent of the claimants, L. S. Suarez, connected with the firm of P. Harmony, Nephews and Co. which dealt in guano, wrote to Clayton, June 7, 1849, proposing that the State Department offer to accept guano from Peru instead of cash in payment of the damage installments. He claimed that Peru had just sent his firm a quantity of guano to be sold in order that the proceeds be applied to a debt which

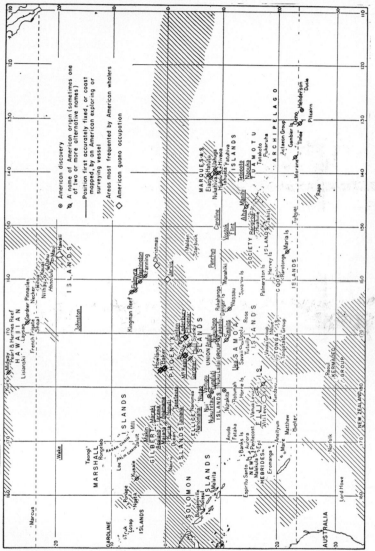

The Islands of the Pacific

Peru owed a foreign house. He furthermore reported that the scheme had the confidential approval of the Peruvian Consul General, Don Juan Ignacio de Osma. Clayton was favorably impressed and sent the proposal to Lima. At that time and for a decade to come, American interests there were in the hands of one of the most capable of our South American representatives, John Randolph Clay, and he immediately sought to further the scheme. He soon found that it was not practical, for not only was it contrary to the terms of the treaty, which specified that the money should be paid in coin at Lima, but Peru had contracted to export guano only through Gibbs and Company. The only ray of hope was the confidential assurance which he received from the Peruvian government that when the Gibbs contract expired in December, the United States market would not be included in a renewal.

Farmers' organizations in Maryland, Delaware and Virginia now began to be heard from in the spring of 1850 and Richard Pollard, a former chargé at Lima and now a Virginia planter, urged that the State Department propose to Peru that she do away with agents and gain revenue by an export duty on guano. Suarez too wrote again citing the arrangement made by British holders of Peruvian bonds whereby half the proceeds of guano sales in England were set aside for their benefit. These proposals were sent on to Clay with instructions to try to negotiate further and in the meantime Clayton determined to act himself as a new Peruvian representative, Don José Manuel Tirado, was about to arrive in Washington.

The circumstances of the coming of Tirado, Clayton considered to be auspicious. A private letter which he had received from Clay that spring had related some interesting news. The pending commercial treaty of 1848 had been rejected recently under peculiar circumstances. Clay reported that the merits of the treaty had hardly entered into the case but that the agreement had been used as the basis for a political intrigue. Tirado, he said, was a local politician of great renown who had been in opposition to the Castilla administration; to placate him and remove him from the field, the plan was made to send him on an important foreign mission. Madrid and Rome were first considered but Congress had failed to provide the money and so the government had procured the rejection of the treaty in order that a mission to the United States could be created and Tirado sent up to make a new treaty. Clay had also reported that the existing arrangement lined the pockets of certain administration politicians and naturally they were averse to change. Tirado on the other hand was of the opposition and presumably not averse to modifying the terms.

Under these circumstances Clayton hoped to make more favorable arrangements. Tirado assured him that Peru was about to change her policy as soon as the mortgage on the guano was paid off and he further showed evidence of a willingness to make concessions by incorporating an article in the new treaty in regard to guano. This article provided that if guano were ever sold by Peru at its own ports, no discriminating duties would be levied against the United States; such a clause was meaningless because other articles in the treaty granted us most-favored-nation privileges and prohibited discrimination. Nevertheless, Clayton thought he had accomplished a good deal for guano.

The Secretary therefore was much displeased when Clay reported that Castilla's anger had been aroused by the mere fact that Tirado had included the word "guano" in the treaty, meaningless as the clause was. The Peruvian President had refused to accept the treaty, since the use of the word would be too dangerous. It would give his opponents an opportunity to charge him with making guano concessions to the United States. The belief became general that Castilla's action had been caused by the interference of British contractors but Clay made out a plausible case to show that this could not have been true.

An even greater blow to agricultural hopes was the announcement of the award of the new contract to Gibbs and Company. In spite of assurances that better arrangements would be made in this new instrument, no improvements were provided. Clay had informed Americans of the opportunity for bidding, especially after the Peruvian Congress, January 25, 1850, authorized a new loan to be secured by the proceeds of the sale of guano in the United States. In response to advertisements, Alsop and Company and Rollin, Thorne and Company of Lima made proposals for the United States agency, and a group of American interests sent down an agent. Robert Soulter, Jr., representing family interests in New York, Philadelphia and Norfolk, by pamphlet writing and lobbying attempted to persuade Peru to sell 50,000 tons of guano to his backers at twenty dollars a ton, five dollars more than the net profit which Peru generally received. It all availed nothing. All of these proposals were rejected; Gibbs and Company supplied the money as usual. The English firm, however, did not receive a renewed contract for the American agency. It was awarded to the Peruvian firm of Barreda Bros. Of this firm, the senior member was a Spaniard who had been naturalized and another member was a brother-in-law of Don Juan Ignacio de Osma, the Peruvian chargé at Washington. Clay reported that Tirado was also interested in this firm. Under such circumstances it did no good to argue that Peru might gain more revenue by other arrangements; the existing state of affairs was profitable and secure to those concerned. Evidently the American farmer must still pay high prices for guano or go without.

## II

The continued high price of guano stimulated search for new supplies of the fertilizer. Various items in the British press began calling attention to the Lobos Islands, which like the Chinchas were located off the coast of Peru though much further northward. British sea captains and merchants put forward the claim that these islands were uninhabited and unclaimed. They asserted that Peru seemingly cared nothing for them and that consequently the guano on them might be removed by anyone. The British government evidently did not share this view but rather frowned on the contention. It refused either to question Peru's authority or to send war vessels to protect such British seekers as might attempt to dig the guano. American business men did not let this news pass unnoticed and a ship captain, James C. Jewett, and his backer and silent partner, a speculative New York merchant, Alfred G. Benson, planned to make a fortune if they could secure government backing. Benson was to become the principal guano operator in the United States and his enterprises were to carry American interests afar.

James C. Jewett, ostensibly acting for himself, wrote June 2, 1852, to Daniel Webster, then Secretary of State, inquiring if it were true that guano might be taken from the Lobos by Americans. Webster replied that this might be done. He considered that these islands quite probably had been discovered by Benjamin Morrell, Jr., an American citizen, in 1823, and therefore Americans had the best right, a right which he would suggest to the Secretary of the Navy should be backed up by naval protection. Webster sent a draft of this reply over to the White House for President Fillmore's approval. In due course it came back endorsed "Approved M.F." in the President's handwriting. Presumably Fillmore gave it little attention for he could never recollect later having endorsed it. Webster thereupon signed it on June 5th but in doing so decided on the spur of the moment to add a postscript in his own hand, "It is considered important that this letter should not be made public at present." Webster had recently been thrown from his carriage and had seriously injured his head, his memory was impaired and he later disclaimed all remembrance of this addition, publicly stating that, whatever its origin, "it did not originate in a desire to give Mr. Jewett or anyone else exclusive information as to the views of the government in regard to those islands." This statement is in part borne out by the fact that he gave somewhat similar information to Magoun and Son of Boston a few days later though he left several other inquiries unanswered. Webster maintained that he had no personal acquaintance with Jewett. True to his promise the Secretary recommended the dispatch of a warship and the Navy Department complied. Jewett who was now in Washington was assured verbally by the Secretary of the Navy that the vessel would be sent, and the captain so wired Benson.

Encouraged by these assurances, preparations began to be made in New York and Boston to launch a speculation. Benson went to work on a large scale and through an agent he began chartering ships and procuring equipment to be sent to the Lobos to remove the guano. He planned to sell the fertilizer at thirty dollars a ton, about forty per cent below the current price, and had dreams of great profits. He advertised in the press for ships, stating that naval protection was assured, and went so far as to make contracts to deliver guano at the low price. Peru, however, was to be reckoned with, the islands belonged to her she claimed, and de Osma, as soon as he heard of Benson's grand scheme, bestirred himself. He saw Webster and the President and lodged vigorous protest. Webster brushed him aside grandly declaring that if the United States were wrong it could easily pay for the guano. In New York Thomas Galway, the Peruvian consul, published a warning to the effect that the islands were Peruvian and under a decree of 1842 all foreign vessels approaching guano islands were liable to seizure and confiscation. Benson's agents replied in the newspaper columns that they were under government protection. Mercantile circles began to wonder and President Fillmore was not quite sure that Webster's policy was correct.

Webster in this the last summer of his life was beset by many ills and disappointments. In May he had been injured, in June he had seen his last hope of a Presidential nomination defeated in the Whig convention, while the summer was always a miserable time because of hay fever. He tried to be at his house in Marshfield as much as possible and left Washington shortly after the first of July, leaving directions for the writing of a reply to de Osma. In due course the chief clerk, William Hunter, sent this reply to Fillmore. The President had been doubtful about our claim to the Lobos and his doubts were confirmed by study of the papers which the ministry had submitted to the British parliament in which it was made quite plain that Great Britain considered that the islands were Peruvian. Fillmore wrote to Webster suggesting modification and Webster agreed to reconsider it. In the meantime he was waxing bellicose with Great Britain over Newfoundland fishing rights.

The strength of the Peruvian case had been ably set forth in the newspapers and the idea seems to have been bruited about that Benson's claim of government protection might be fictitious. To quiet these innuendoes presumably, Jewett now published his letter from Webster. It saw the light of print at a bad time, for the State Department had just received a long report from Clay.

Our Peruvian chargé knew nothing of recent events in the United States, nothing of Webster's position, and he reported as though he were contributing to his superiors their first knowledge of the Lobos guano possibilities. He sought to demolish what he thought was the British claim that the Lobos were nobody's islands. Quite without question they belonged to Peru and if the United States did not uphold Peru's claim, the British would very likely seize the islands for themselves. With this clear proof of the incorrectness of Webster's contentions before him, Fillmore was much agitated to see the Jewett letter in print.

How had Webster dared to write such a letter without his approval? He went over to the State Department to see Webster who had recently returned for what proved to be his last sojourn in the capital. Fillmore inspected the correspondence, the letter was there but with no postscript or sign of Presidential approval. It had never been folded and such papers were always sealed in envelopes when sent over to the Executive Mansion. Webster was sure that the President had approved the letter but there was no evidence and Fillmore denied any recollection of it. Only after Webster died was part of the mystery cleared up. His son found a number of State Department papers at Marshfield which his father had neglected to return, among them was a draft of the Jewett letter approved by the President; this draft too had no postscript. The whole thing exasperated

Fillmore for it was not the first time his great Secretary had embarrassed him. Webster's speech at the Kossuth dinner and his recent fireworks over the fisheries now were followed by this grandiloquent Lobos gesture. It was too much. Newspapers announced that Peru had seized the islands and was determined to hold them. Great Britain held that the islands were Peruvian. Clay who knew more about it than anyone else said that the islands belonged to Peru. To the President's mind there was nothing left but to back down.

Webster did not reverse himself without some attempt to bolster his claim. He tried to take advantage of the offer of his friend Hiram Ketchum to procure evidence of the "actual occupancy, the undisturbed possession" which Webster had claimed that the United States had enjoyed over the islands for the last fifty years through the frequent visits of whalers and seal-catchers. Ketchum scouted out old whalers who sent in their testimony, and a few papers tried to make out a case, but to no avail. Reports came from New York that the uncertainty was making the affair a mask for fraud. Ship captains were seeking charter parties so they could have the basis for a claim against the government if they got into the expected trouble at the Lobos. Webster may also have learned of the connection between Jewett and Benson and that Benson was no friend of his, while the firms dealing with the Peruvian guano agents were.

In spite of Ketchum's whalers and Morrell's *Voyages,* Webster had to yield to the President. So in his last public paper he replied to de Osma on August 21st and the President sent the papers to Congress. Webster still refused to admit absolutely that he had been wrong, but said that he was willing to accept further evidence from de Osma and in the meantime the United States naval protection would be withdrawn; he hoped there would be no collision. He wrote to Jewett informing him that Peru claimed these islands and under the circumstances protection must be denied. Orders were sent recalling the war vessels and Clay was instructed to continue his efforts to secure a reduction in price and to obtain from Peru a permission for vessels which had left the United States in good faith between June 1st and August 24th to bring back a load of guano each. With this instruction, Webster laid down the Lobos, taking full responsibility for the letter of June 5th and its consequences. Three days later he left Washington for the last time and Charles M. Conrad, Secretary of War, assumed temporary charge of the State Department.

In Peru meanwhile there had been much apprehension for it was widely believed that the United States was planning to capture the islands. The Peruvian government was therefore anxious to forestall such action and was ready to bargain with the United States for the recognition of their ownership. So before Webster's change of policy was known, an experienced diplomat, Don Joaquin José de Osma, brother of the chargé at Washington, was sent to Washington armed with power to make concessions. This appointment Clay duly reported in a dispatch dated August 7th and gave the information that he believed if the United States would recognize Peru's title, she would charter the ships which had already sailed to carry guano back to the United States. When they delivered the guano to the Peruvian agents, the shipmasters would be paid a freight charge several dollars per ton higher than usual. When this dispatch arrived on September 16th, Conrad immediately notified Jewett, who had been clamoring for redress, as well as others who had sent ships to Peru. He told them that the Department expected that the arrangement described by Clay would be put into effect.

The elder de Osma appeared on the scene September 21st and presented his letters of credence, then he left for New York without so much as a hint at negotiations. Such conduct was to say the least unusual. According to Benson who was much disgruntled at the way in which the government had reversed itself and left his ships on the high seas without protection, the explanation of de Osma's move was simple. Both the de Osma brothers, so Benson said, were interested in guano; in fact one of the Barreda brothers who held the American concession was a brother-in-law of the younger diplomat. When the elder arrived and found that the United States had reversed itself, he felt that there was no longer any need for much concession, as the State Department seemed only too glad to get out of the scrape caused by Webster's rashness. Therefore, he intended to let the United States do the coaxing and went off to New York where he stayed until Conrad ordered him back September 28th.

When de Osma at length returned, he submitted a note but instead of making a proposition, he contented himself with making a long statement of Peru's claim to the islands. Thereupon Conrad returned with a practical demand that the vessels in question be permitted to take guano on their own account, claiming that Clay's reported concession offered by the Peruvian government would bring no recompense to those who had contracts to deliver guano at prices below the market. The next page in the story of the negotiations has disappeared, namely a letter which de Osma wrote on October 25th. Its contents were such, however, as to cause Conrad to accuse de Osma of saying one thing and later changing it when he put it in writing. He concluded his note of November 1st as follows: "What the Undersigned now wishes to know is, whether he is to understand from Mr. de Osma's note that the proposition contained in it, is the only one he is prepared to make on this subject. To this question an early and categorical answer is respectfully requested."

This was Conrad's last act, for at that point a new director appeared. Webster had just died and Edward Everett was appointed to succeed him. He arrived at his new post to find both parties diplomatically offended and the negotiations at a standstill. Everett gave the case immediate attention and after several days of negotiating directly with de Osma, he received the approval of the President and cabinet on terms agreed upon. The United States recognized Peru's sovereignty over the islands and in return the Peruvian government agreed to freight all the vessels that had sailed under proper charter party between the dates mentioned, paying them a freight charge of twenty dollars a ton or four dollars more than the usual payment. The said freight was to be delivered to Peruvian agents in the United States or Europe on Peru's account; furthermore Peru would buy the guano equipment which the American merchants had acquired. Finally de Osma was to withdraw his note of October 25th and Everett would call back Conrad's reply of November 1st. The speculators who had hoped for great profits were disappointed and unfortunate difficulties about freight and equipment purchase ensued, but bloodshed was avoided and the United States was free from the stigma of an attempt to overawe a weaker neighbor. Everett's act also saved Peru from bankruptcy and revolution, for had he persisted the Chincha concession would have proved of much less value and Peru would have lost her borrowing power.

When Marcy succeeded Everett in March, 1853, he

studied the guano situation carefully and finally instructed Clay to try as usual to reduce the price. But Peru was in the throes of revolution during most of the years of Marcy's rule, and no results came. Clay suggested that United States buy the Chincha Islands and one of the Peruvian politicians suggested that a new arrangement might be made if the United States guaranteed Peru's title to the Chinchas and made a loan of from three to five million dollars. Nothing came of all these matters—guano must be bought from other sources. Benson tried to get damages but a claims commission finally disallowed them a decade later.

## III

As Marcy was writing failure across the account of his efforts to gain Peruvian guano concessions, word came of a new source of supply. Seven days' voyage from Guayaquil, Ecuador, amid the wastes of the Pacific, lie the Galápagos Islands, so far away from human habitation as sometimes to be called World's End. The Republic of Ecuador had claimed these sea orphans and had farmed them out to one of her revolutionary leaders. Gen. José Villamil, a native of New Orleans, had been prominent in aiding Ecuador to gain independence and thereafter he had conceived the idea of colonizing the Galápagos. The grateful republic had granted them to himself and some associates but the colony had not prospered. At this particular time, Villamil was Ecuadorian chargé at Washington and he was by no means unaware of the value of guano. His Galápagos Islands, if they contained such deposits, would at last prove valuable, so he undertook to find out. He hired an American steamship captain, a citizen of New Orleans, Captain Julius de Brissot, to explore for him, promising him that he should receive some of the royalties belonging to the discoverer of hidden treasure if his efforts were successful.

In the spring of 1854 de Brissot returned to New Orleans and his report caused Villamil to leave Washington for that city. The captain told him that he had discovered eleven deposits, one of great size; he had buried evidence of his visit and had brought back samples of a guano equal in quality to that of the Chincha Islands. Villamil acted immediately. De Brissot was to write to the State Department announcing his discovery and asking the protection of his government for his rights; Senator Judah P. Benjamin was to act as his counsel before the Department. Villamil himself would report the matter to the Ecuadorian government and set off for home to protect his rights there. The plan was carried out. De Brissot wrote Marcy on May 23rd inclosing a letter from Villamil endorsing his claim. Benjamin took the matter up at the State Department and Marcy invited de Brissot to come to Washington at government expense to report his discovery.

Marcy went over the whole matter carefully with Benjamin and de Brissot and at length made up his mind to act. Everything must be done that could be, to procure this supply of guano for the exclusive use of the United States. To this end he drew up instructions to the American chargé at Quito, Philo White, and sent them down in Benjamin's care. Benjamin's ostensible object would be to negotiate a contract with the Ecuadorian government protecting de Brissot's rights as a discoverer. We may presume that he was also commissioned to help White negotiate for exclusive American privileges. White was directed to secure the right for Americans to take all the guano on the islands "at a specified sum to be paid as it shall be taken away," the sum to be one or two dollars a ton or perhaps a little more. Also, the United States was to seek the right to protect its citizens against intrusions or depredations. To induce the Ecuadorian government more readily to grant this concession, White was authorized to offer a loan of two or three hundred thousand dollars to be gradually refunded and he might even offer to buy the islands for two or three million dollars. If he could gain no exclusive privileges he was to see that the United States paid no more than any other nations for the guano and was to secure de Brissot's rights as discoverer. At all events, White was to reach no agreements until he had sent someone to the islands to confirm the existence of valuable guano deposits.

In the meantime Ecuador was moved with a strange excitement. The Ecuadorians well knew what a gold mine the guano islands had proven to the Peruvian government and now the arrival of Villamil with the news that a similar treasure belonged to Ecuador filled many, especially the ruling officials, with high hopes. Already American merchants were seeking concessions and the politicians could almost see the gold in their coffers. The President and the foreign minister went to Guayaquil where they commissioned the American consul, Captain Game, to go with Villamil and investigate the Galápagos deposits.

All did not run smoothly, however, and there was cause for wonder. Just as Marcy's instructions arrived Captain Game returned. His most careful search, urged on by Villamil's hopes, had been unable to find any guano on the Galápagos. But the hope was too bright to be immediately dispelled, the Islands were numerous, de Brissot's samples had been proof positive of some location. While waiting for further developments, let the negotiations proceed. White reported that it was a favorable time to treat in view of the uncertainty. "Under present discouragements, this government may be disposed to grant liberal concessions to those willing to incur the expense of making still further exploitations." White and Benjamin both went to work. White invited proposals from the Ecuadorian government but soon discovered that the foreign office would do nothing until Benjamin had succeeded in making a three-cornered arrangement in regard to the rights of de Brissot and Villamil to royalties as discoverers. After the usual delay, Benjamin got a contract signed whereby a fifth of the guano was allotted to the discoverers; of this amount Villamil was to have two-thirds and de Brissot one-third. Now President Urbina was willing to listen to White. In the ensuing negotiations Benjamin was of great help to the American representative who found him "possessed of extraordinary tact and maturity of judgment as well as of a very high order of talent. Although impelled by a personal interest in the enterprise to obtain the best terms for the discoverers, yet his patriotism and magnanimity prompted him to exert his influence in favor of the most liberal treaty stipulations in securing supplies of guano to our countrymen at large on the best terms practicable."

In spite of White's generous estimate of Benjamin the negotiations were not very successful. After much bargaining a treaty was signed, but such a treaty! In return for a loan of $3,000,000 to be paid back from the proceeds of guano sales, the United States was to be permitted to buy guano at a price of one dollar per ton less than that collected from other purchasers. This reduced price was to be in effect until the loan was repaid. The treaty was achieved, it seems, largely because Ecuador wanted American protection for her possessions. Immediately after the news of the treaty was announced, the diplomatic representatives of England, France, Spain and Peru called upon the Ecuadorian government and unceremoniously denounced them for making this agreement.

Meanwhile, White hired Emile Prats who had come from New Orleans with Benjamin to go to the Galápagos to see if he could not find the guano which de Brissot had described. The Ecuadorian government placed a revenue cutter at his disposal and Benjamin and Villamil went with him. Their journey to the islands was entirely fruitless and after searching in vain they went on to the United States. Benjamin presented the treaty to the President and to Marcy, January 11, 1855, but at the same time he was forced to report that in all probability there was no guano anywhere in Ecuador. Marcy never even acknowledged the treaty and White was forced to conclude that it was just "an adroit scheme preconceived by the derelict individual," de Brissot. No one has ever been able to find any guano on the Galápagos.

## IV

Alfred G. Benson had not been discouraged by his unfortunate experience in Peru and was turning to greater efforts in a far distant quarter of the globe. The continued high price of guano and the immense profit if a cheap supply could be found, led Benson to undertake a speculation in far distant waters. There were guano islands in Polynesia and a new impulse was given American enterprise to enter the Pacific.

Whalers from Nantucket and New Bedford had often sighted barren bird rookeries in the Phoenix, Gilbert, Ellice and Caroline Islands, which they called the Kingsmill whaling grounds of Polynesia. They had paid little attention to them save to land occasionally in search of eggs with which to freshen their diet. Some of these isles had been named, such as New Nantucket, 0° 13′ N. Lat., 176° 33′ W. Long., but most of them were nameless and many uncharted. In the 1820's, the pattern of future American interest could be traced when the whaling fleets were joined by the first Pacific squadron of the Navy and a consul appeared in the Hawaiian Islands. Whalers sometimes got into trouble in these waters with rivals under other flags and in 1828 a petition came from Nantucket for protection. The Navy Department saw the need of information and that same year, the Secretary commissioned J. N. Reynolds to visit the whalers in the New England ports to secure reliable data on these distant and confusing, often uncharted, islets. After a summer's work, talking to sailors and examining ships' logs, he filed a report. He had discovered 178 voyages through Polynesian waters and recorded that American captains had visited a number of islands which had been given names, including New Nantucket, Howland, Canton, Palmyra and others which were later to become objects of controversy.

In the next decade, another Secretary of the Navy sent Reynolds' report to Congress and ordered Captain Charles Wilkes to undertake an extensive exploring expedition in Polynesia with a fleet of war vessels. The government wanted accurate knowledge for the benefit of the whaling industry and when Wilkes came back in 1842 after four years of investigating and charting, his observations were published by Congress in a series of volumes. Map makers were becoming accustomed to labeling the Kingsmill whaling ground as American Polynesia. It was in this region that Benson undertook to establish a profitable business and to destroy the British monopoly.

Benson realized that he must be in a position to invoke the aid of government, if the need arose, so he was careful to provide evidence of his interest and operation. First according to time-honored procedure, he must establish "discoverer's rights." Captain Edward W. Turner of the *Star of the West* had knowledge of these waters and could give evidence. He and Captain Thomas D. Lucas of New Bedford, designated as attorney for an ancient mariner, Michael Baker of South Dartmouth, Massachusetts, arranged a documentary set-up which Benson thought would be the legal basis for insuring government protection of his new guano business if the need arose. Baker was ready to swear that in 1832 he had "discovered" two islands practically on the equator, one of them, already known as New Nantucket, was hereafter to be designated Baker Island and the second was Jarvis, thirteen hundred miles to the east, 0° 22' S. Lat., 160° 0' W. Long. Baker stated in his affidavit that he had made various visits to these islands in the years that followed and in 1839 while commanding the *Gideon Howland* had buried a sailor on Baker.

Baker's attorney, Lucas, executed an agreement with Turner in March, 1855, whereby he disposed of Baker's "rights" to Turner for $25,000 to be paid if these islands were proved to have guano deposits upon them. Benson then wrote to President Pierce, May 5, 1855, calling his attention "to the discovery by an American citizen of a barren and uninhabited island" containing 200,000,000 tons of guano. He wished to inquire whether the United States would protect the discoverers of this island, the location of which Benson carefully refrained from indicating. No reply to this letter is on record. Benson and Turner became partners and in September the American Guano Company was organized to whom Benson and Turner sold Baker Island.

The American Guano Company was a New York corporation capitalized at $1,000,000 divided into 100,000 shares of $10 each. Turner was assigned 30,000 shares, Benson 29,930 shares and seven friends of the latter, ten each. The remaining 40,000 shares were to be held in the treasury to be used for promotion purposes. Alfred G. Benson was elected president, Bertram H. Howell, vice president, and James S. Wyckoff, secretary and treasurer. The headquarters of the company were at Benson's offices, 39 South Street, New York City.

The new corporation took elaborate pains to secure assurance of government protection. Definite evidence of possession was necessary so Turner was authorized to charter a ship with company funds and proceed to Baker where he was to create some proof of occupation. He sailed from San Francisco on the *Kalima,* December 7, 1855, and in January reached Jarvis. Here he landed and built a house in which he left evidence of occupation. Then he proceeded to Baker but so stormy was the weather and so high the sea that he found it impossible to make a landing. Also he saw vegetation on the island and this he felt probably meant that no guano was there. So he turned homeward.

While Turner was thus engaged Benson and his business associates proceeded to Washington in October, 1855, to present a memorial to President Pierce and James C. Dobbin, his Secretary of the Navy, asking for some form of naval investigation to confirm or disprove the existence of guano on these islands. The President and the Secretary agreed to send a warship to explore. On October 20, 1855, Dobbin instructed Commodore Mervine of the Pacific squadron to dispatch a vessel "with a view to ascertaining the correctness of the information, of protecting our citizens in their rights and taking care of the interests of our country." An agent of the company was to carry these orders to Mervine and to accompany the expedition at the company's expense. So George W. Benson, half brother of Alfred G. Benson, was given the papers to deliver to Commodore Mervine at San Francisco who was directed to permit Benson to accompany the expedition.

Benson went to San Francisco via Panama where he arrived November 25th, a week before Turner sailed. Mervine was so interested that he decided to go himself and they sailed on January 18, 1856. They stopped at the Hawaiian and Navigator's Islands where reports were adverse. The local people claimed there was no guano on these islands. When they arrived at New Nantucket or Baker Island, the weather was bad and the Commodore became convinced of the "utter impossibility [of landing] beating to windward against a trade wind and a strong current." As he was already certain that there was no guano he refused to let Benson and a volunteer crew try a landing. Also he saw no use in going to Jarvis Island. Consequently he sailed back to Valparaiso where he wrote an adverse report, June 30, 1856.

The company had proceeded to complete formalities while the naval expedition was at work. A second ship, the *Corea,* had been chartered at an expense of ten thousand shares of stock from Lucas, Baker's attorney. He was to sail this ship, accompanied by Theodore Lewis, the company's agent. Lucas and Lewis were to attest the existence of Turner's evidences of occupation and take over the islands for the American Guano Company. They sailed from Talcahuano, Chile, January 11, 1856, following Turner by five weeks. They accomplished their mission at Jarvis but at Baker they had no better luck than Turner or Mervine. They could not land. Perhaps because word had been received that Baker might not possess guano, or that landing on it was impractical, Benson and Turner's attorney, Oscar

Coles, gave title to Jarvis Island to the American Guano Company. There may have been other reasons for this transaction, as the date of the instrument, February 25, 1856, would seem to be earlier than any report of Turner's difficulty at Baker, which occurred January 16th, might have arrived at New York. The American Guano Company had thus created the legal bases of property rights. They had deeds from the assignees of a discoverer and they had witnesses to occupation by them of these properties. If conclusive testimony was supplied by the Navy, the flag of the United States would soon be flying in the Pacific.

## V

The demand for fertilizer created renewed interest in nearer waters. The Caribbean had its own myriad of bird-perched islets and the quest for guano gave them their first importance. Here, likewise, ship captains played their role. Mariners in the employ of Boston firms had been keeping a weather eye out for strange isles with treasures of bird lime. Sampson and Tappan and Philo S. Shelton on the one hand and Lang and Delano, New England merchants, were hopeful of profit from anticipated discoveries. Captain Nathan P. Gibbs, sailing for the first of these firms, was successful in March, 1854, in locating a supply on Aves Island, about one hundred miles distant from the nearest island in the West Indies and more than three hundred miles from the mainland of South America. On his way home he told another captain, James Wheeler, employed by the same company, then working a poor deposit on another island, Arenas. Both of these captains expected to be sent to Aves but when Gibbs was preferred and Wheeler saw that his was not to be the chance, he straightway went to Lang and

Delano, who provided him with a ship. The result of this bargaining was the arrival of both Gibbs and Wheeler at Aves on the same day, July 15th, 1854. A quarrel ensued as to which party had the right to take off guano. Discretion seemed the better part of valor to both sides and the captains agreed to divide the island between them. The digging of guano commenced forthwith.

News of this discovery awakened the interest of some Philadelphians and Louis C. Levin, John Tucker, Dr. D. Luther, J. F. D. Wallace and others began to arrange a venture. The island in question though three hundred miles off the coast of Venezuela had been a part of the same Spanish province in colonial days and on that ground Venezuela might claim it now. These speculators decided to send down an agent to obtain a guano contract from Venezuela for the Philadelphia Guano Company which they planned to incorporate. Their initial efforts were successful. In December, 1854, Wallace arrived in Venezuela and a few days later a Venezuelan gunboat sailed off to Aves. The captain ordered the Bostonian agents to leave, though as a concession he permitted them to load up. In the course of negotiations the representatives of the Boston firms signed a paper written in Spanish which acknowledged Venezuelan ownership. Whether the Americans knew enough Spanish to understand what they were signing is doubtful; nevertheless, the paper remained to haunt them.

Immediately after the return of the Venezuelan naval force, Wallace signed a contract permitting the Philadelphia interest to take guano at four dollars a ton. In return for this privilege Venezuela might draw upon John Tucker for $200,000 in ninety-day notes; the contract was not to be binding until Tucker accepted the drafts. Furthermore, the

American guano operators were to aid Venezuela in protecting Aves from foreign invasion.

The Boston firms turned immediately to the State Department for redress and Marcy instructed our representative at Caracas, Charles Eames, to investigate. His inquiries and protests at the Venezuelan foreign office were met with a display of the paper signed by the American agents acknowledging Venezuelan ownership. In such a case, Eames was at a loss how to proceed and waited for Marcy to instruct him further. When the Secretary received this report he took the Boston people to task for not apprising him fully of the acts of their agents and was inclined to consider the case hopeless.

Scarcely a week after Marcy had laid aside the Boston claim an agent from the Philadelphia firm waited upon him with a grievance. The Venezuelan government had annulled their contract for the ostensible reason that Tucker had refused to accept the drafts. It seemed that there had been delay in organizing the Philadelphia company and it had not been incorporated until April 30th. The drafts had been presented in the meantime and as no funds had been paid in, Tucker refused to risk his personal credit by accepting them. The Company was ready to pay these obligations by July 4th when they were due, but in spite of that fact the Venezuelan government had refused to wait and had annulled their contract. We may suspect that one cause of this action was the fact that the minister preferred the advantage of making one of his own. At any rate, that was not then known and the Philadelphia agent was asking Marcy to secure redress. Marcy saw that there was danger of British or Dutch interference and the consequent loss of any chance for American exploitation of this guano. He, therefore, took an unusual course to help out the Philadelphia firm.

Not only did he instruct Eames to take the usual steps but he ordered him to help the agent, John F. Pickrell, to secure a renewal of the contract. He wrote him a private letter as well as a public instruction and gave the agent a semi-official character as bearer of dispatches. While he cautioned Eames not to use "minatory language," he made it clear that the maintenance of the Philadelphia contract was "of great public importance to the people of the United States." Eames and Pickrell worked effectively together and, as the Venezuelan government later complained, with unusual vigor. Eames perhaps forgot the prohibition of minority language. The result was a new contract of September 29, 1855, whereby the Philadelphia Guano Company received the exclusive right to take guano at five dollars a ton. Eames was much pleased with the result and the Guano company began to dig. It seemed at length as though there was a supply which could be controlled by Americans.

# 10. The Birth of Empire

GUANO prospecting was introducing a new type of exasperation into the relations between government and private enterprise. The State and Navy Departments had attempted to deal with complaints of trespass and disregard of rights but had been able to develop neither satisfactory solutions nor effective procedures largely because there was no legal sanction for such action. The guano operators began to demand some law which would create procedures not dependent upon the whims of Secretaries.

The Boston firms interested in Aves had been incensed at Marcy's willingness to help their Philadelphia rivals and began significant pressure on him. They stressed the point particularly that their agents had signed the renunciation in ignorance of its meaning. They at length prevailed upon Marcy to believe he was wrong and persuaded him to aid them in securing damages. But in the meantime, they turned to Congress with a demand for legislation to provide for regular procedure. There must be some way provided whereby the United States government might recognize Americans as having rights of occupation which could be made the legal basis for diplomatic protest and protection.

In the spring of 1856 Henry S. Sanford, attorney for Sampson and Tappan and Philo S. Shelton, memorialized Congress to enact a statute. He proposed a draft which would provide that in case an American citizen should find and occupy a guano island that the "right of sovereignty and eminent domain of, to and over the same" would be vested in the United States and the government would have the power to protect Americans in its use by force of arms. This petition for Congressional action might not have produced much of a ripple, had not allies appeared in Washington lobbies to join the effort for legislation.

Like these Aves claimants, Benson and his associates operating in the Pacific were aware of the fact that there was no law to protect their "property rights." They now turned to Congress, where Sanford was already laboring. They sent their counsel, George Wood, to Washington with a petition for a bill which he presented in May. They also began to work on individual Senators and Representatives. Edwin Croswell who was prominent in Democratic party councils wrote friends, including Senator Douglas, and Benson who seems to have been a Republican got to work through Seward. Congress had heretofore not given much attention to the subject of guano. Several calls for papers had been made in connection with the Peruvian and Venezuelan difficulties, and in response to petitions from Maryland and Delaware farmers, the House in the previous Congress had raised a special committee to study the subject. The committee reported in due time endorsing a bill to levy tariff duties on Peruvian guano in such fashion as practically to prohibit its importation unless the price was lowered. The House, however, took no action. Now, the Senate had the Sampson and Tappan bill before it; but more important, Senator Seward, May 26, 1856, introduced the bill sponsored by the American Guano Company. The new bill provided not only for the protection of discoverers but also sought to make financial inducements to encourage merchants to search for new islands.

Congress was favorably inclined and after little debate

in the Senate and none in the House the Seward bill became the law of August 18, 1856.* Now discoverers by following the procedure outlined in the act could register their finds and obtain official recognition in their rights, provided no other nation could established a claim to the guano in question. Islands so registered became a part of the United States so long as their guano deposits lasted. The government insured to the discoverer the exclusive right to take and sell the guano and established the price at either four dollars or eight dollars a ton, the latter if delivered on board the vessel. Sales might be made to American citizens only. The discoverers or their representatives must give bond, in such penalty and with such sureties as the President might require, to deliver the guano to citizens of the United States only, and for use therein, at the price prescribed, and to provide all necessary facilities for that purpose within a fixed time. When these formalities were completed to the satisfaction of the President, these islands would be "considered as appertaining to the United States."

## II

Now that the act was passed, efforts were stepped up to mobilize the Atlantic supply. While the Philadelphia Guano Company was continuing its operations on Aves, some of their less fortunate neighbors attempted to invoke the new act for protection. John E. Gowan and Franklin Copeland had been endeavoring to take guano from other Venezuelan Islands, Las Monges (The Monks), but had been driven off in 1855 while the Aves trouble was flourishing.

* The Boston operators, besides promoting this bill, pushed their claim for damages. The Buchanan Administration accepted their contention and settlement was provided by treaty of January 14, 1859. The total of $639,412 was scaled down to $130,000.

Now they made a new claim which they sought to file according to the procedure laid down in the Act of 1856. They produced an affidavit that one of their captains, Mettiah Jordan, had discovered guano on Sombrero Island, east of the Virgin Islands in the West Indies. Likewise they filed a bond dated February 23, 1857, and an affidavit that they had taken possession of the island December 1, 1856, and had since been working it. Shortly thereafter, Joseph W. Fabens, a Democratic politician who had held various minor diplomatic posts in Latin America, wrote to the State Department in May reporting that he had discovered several large deposits on Caribbean islands, particularly on the Swan Islands, considerably to the north of Honduras. He and his associates desired to fit out an expedition for the purpose of occupying these islands and he wanted an official statement of procedure.

The appearance of these claimants caused the Buchanan Administration to take up the act of 1856 and study its meaning. Attorney-General Black gave his opinion June 2, 1857, on the rules which should be laid down. He prescribed that certain facts must be established by those wishing the benefit of the act, namely, that an American citizen had discovered guano upon an island not occupied or within the lawful jurisdiction of another government and that he had taken and kept peaceful possession thereof in the name of the United States. When the President was satisfied as to these points and an acceptable bond was filed he might "in his discretion, regard the islands . . . as belonging to the United States."

Fabens and associates who were ready to work the Swan Islands now endeavored to follow these rules. Furthermore, Fabens requested a warship be sent in like manner as others had been dispatched in the Pacific to Baker and Jarvis.

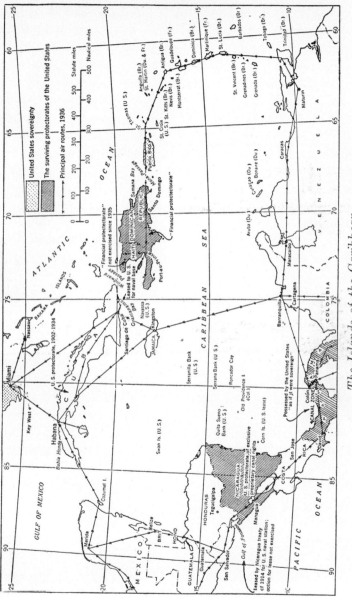

The Islands of the Caribbean

However, neither group could satisfy the State Department, so they both proceeded without government certificates. Wood and Grant advertised in 1858 that Sombrero had the richest deposit of Phosphate of Lime known in the world which they offered at thirty dollars a ton, half the Peruvian price.* Fabens, Charles Stearns and Duff Green organized the Atlantic and Pacific Guano Company which operated the Swan Islands deposits and also the Aves works after the short-lived Philadelphia Guano Company abandoned them sometime in 1858.†

So far in the Atlantic, the procedure had been independent and individual; not much attention had been paid to the Act of 1856. Now for the first time a regular procedure was to be followed in the case of the island of Navassa. On July 1, 1857, Captain Peter Duncan, so he swore, found guano in quantity on that sea dot. Navassa was a barren isle, shaped like an oyster shell, about a square mile in area, formed of volcanic limestone and so filled with holes as to have the appearance of a petrified sponge. It was situated some thirty miles west of Haiti, 18° 10′ N. Lat., 75° W. Long., about seventy-five east of Jamaica. Captain Duncan found it unoccupied and covered with an amount of guano which he estimated at one million tons. He took possession in the name of the United States and upon his return home assigned his discoverer's rights to Captain E. O. Cooper. The latter and Edward K. Cooper of Baltimore, who seems to have been the business agent, sent John B.

* The bond dated February 23, 1857, for Sombrero, though disapproved by Black, was kept on file and when the official list of Guano Islands was published August 23, 1867, Sombrero was included.

† In 1862, the Atlantic and Pacific Company sold its interest in the Swan Islands to the New York Guano Company. This company filed a bond dated December 30, 1862, and Seward issued a certificate to them in lieu of a proclamation, February 11, 1863.

Lewis to the island to work the guano deposit and filed formal notice of the discovery at the State Department on December 3, 1857, without supplying either the required certificate of peaceable possession or the bond.

Cooper had once had a partner in the guano trade, a Jamaican, Ramoth by name, with whom he had broken, as it was later reported, because of Ramoth's inefficiency. The latter had harbored a desire to get even and now saw his chance. He went to Port-au-Prince, suggested to the Emperor that the island belonged to Haiti and obtained a lease of the island, contracting to give the government one-third of the proceeds of any guano sales. The new lease-holder then went to the governor of Jamaica and told him that Americans were taking Ramoth's guano. The Jamaican executive promptly gave him a letter to the Emperor of Haiti supporting a request for a war vessel to protect this Haitian island from American invasion. E. K. Cooper learned of this and hastened to complete the formalities connected with filing evidence in the State Department. He presented an affidavit of peaceable possession which Lewis had made recently and on April 23rd warned the Secretary of State that the Haitian government might interfere.

The Emperor of Haiti acted early in June and sent two vessels to order the Americans off his island of Navassa. Cooper turned immediately to President Buchanan and Secretary Cass for protection with the result that a frigate was ordered to proceed to the scene. In spite of a second hostile expedition, the Americans stuck to their digging until Commander Turner arrived on the *Saratoga* in August. He found that the visiting officers had attempted nothing violent; nevertheless he deemed it wise to go to Port-au-Prince to give formal notice that the United States would protect American guano diggers under the law of 1856.

The Haitian government meanwhile had become acquainted with Ramoth's real motives. Under the circumstances, the Emperor was not disposed to get into trouble with the United States just to satisfy the contractor's revenge and even without Turner's show of force would probably have refrained from violent action. The Negro potentate contented himself with filing a protest through the Haitian commercial agent in the United States, B. C. Clark of Boston. The latter claimed Navassa for Haiti on the ground that the island in question had belonged first to Spain and then to France during the colonial era and had been acknowledged to be Haitian when the French recognized the independence of their erstwhile colony.

John Appleton, Assistant Secretary of State, replied, November 17, 1858, that the department had proof that the island was abandoned and derelict when Duncan discovered it and that the United States intended to protect its citizens in taking guano. Appleton concluded, though, with the statement "the act does not make obligatory upon the government to retain permanent possession of the island." As Cooper had filed the required bond on December 8, 1859, Cass at length issued the first guano island proclamation declaring that the required notice of the discovery of guano and the occupation of Navassa in the name of the United States had been filed in the State Department, and that Cooper was "entitled, in respect to the guano on the said island, to all the privileges and advantages intended by that act to be secured to citizens of the United States who may have discovered deposits of guano." Thus Navassa might now be considered as appertaining to the United States. In this humble fashion, the American nation took its first step into the path of imperialism; Navassa, a guano island, was the first noncontiguous territory to be announced formally as attached to the republic.

## III

The Pacific operators had sought to take more immediate advantage of the new law, even before their Atlantic competitors. The American Guano Company hastened to take steps to comply with it. They filed an affidavit from Baker in which he detailed his discovery of the island named for him. As no one had yet succeeded in landing on it, that was as far as they could go. Regarding Jarvis, they could be more explicit. The Company presented statements by Turner that he had visited the atoll and built a house upon it, and by Lewis and Lucas that they had found Turner's house on the island. These papers were accompanied by a chemical analysis of the guano made by A. A. Hayes, Assayer to the State of Massachusetts. Wyckoff, the treasurer of the company, took the papers to Washington in September 1856, to file them and to find out how large a bond would have to be offered. Marcy and Pierce came to the conclusion that $100,000 for each island was the proper figure, so bonds for these sums were provided and deposited with Marcy on November 7, 1856. For some reason, Marcy issued no proclamation recognizing the American Guano Company's rights.

The business prospects of the Benson associates suffered a setback almost at the moment of the filing of their papers. Early in September, Mervine's unfavorable report was published in the press. George W. Benson had returned previously so they knew what to expect and they were prepared to act. G. W. Benson had an article published in the *Journal of Commerce* describing Mervine's failure to investigate properly. The political guns of the associates were brought to bear upon the Pierce Administration to send a second expedition to make a real survey. This was finally arranged in the last hours of Dobbin's authority and Captain Lewis was permitted to sail with the new expedition. In the meantime, Alfred G. Benson's son, Arthur, was sent out with the equipment necessary to dig guano and bring home a cargo. Likewise, he was to prove that Baker could be landed on. He and Charles H. Judd left Honolulu on the *Liholiho*, Christmas day, 1856, and visited Jarvis, Baker and another island, Howland, of which more later. He took formal possession and began the digging of guano. Young Benson returned late in April, 1857, with a hundred tons of guano, most of it on the ship *Illinois*, and the press announced that it was better than Peruvian. Benson also reported that he had experienced no difficulty in landing on Baker Island, thus contradicting Mervine's judgment.

The second naval expedition now set out for these islands in the summer. Commander Charles H. Davis in the U.S.S. *St. Marys* with Captain Lewis on board arrived at Jarvis Island and on August 16, 1857, took formal possession of it for the United States and surveyed its waters. Eight days later Davis reached Baker Island and repeated the formalities. He had no difficulty in landing. However, he was not impressed by the guano on either island which he thought was only soil. He took samples which he dispatched to the Navy Department with his report. By December, 1857, news of the results of the Davis mission were in the press. Little attention was paid to the adverse views of the captain regarding the guano because chemists had analyzed what Arthur Benson had brought home and pronounced it excellent. Their printed testimony was used as advertising by the American Guano Company. Also in May, 1858, the Smithsonian reported on Davis' samples and reversed his judgment. The islands did possess guano though it was probably not as good as Peruvian. All this testimony was securing a market and the American Guano Company prepared to supply it. They made contracts with one of their own directors, William H. Webb, to dig the guano and bring it to the United States for sale. When their supplies began to come in during the winter of 1858–1859, it sold from thirty-two to forty dollars a ton while Peruvian cost sixty dollars.

The American Guano Company soon found itself faced with competition. Another sea captain appeared, William H. Parker, with a lawyer, Richard F. Ryan, laying claim to have discovered some islands visited as early as December 14, 1807, by the British vessel, the *Cornwallis*. Parker declared he had "discovered" six islands, some 600 miles southwest of Hawaii, named Johnston, after the captain of the *Cornwallis,* Cornwallis, Agnes, Ryan, Morrison and Parker, 16° 46′ N. Lat., 169° 17′ W. Long. Parker and Ryan had induced certain speculators, Byxbee and Stoddard, to send their schooner, *Palestine,* to take possession of the islands in the interest of the four of them and join them in working the deposits. Captain Parriman of the *Palestine* took possession of Johnston March 2, 1858 and secured guano samples. The necessary affidavits of discovery and possession were sent to the State Department together with guano samples and were duly acknowledged. On June 9th, Parker, Ryan, Byxbee and Stoddard incorporated the Pacific Guano Company under the laws of California.

The guano business was apt to be a dirty one as was almost immediately demonstrated. While working with Byxbee and Stoddard, Ryan wrote the State Department enclosing Parker's affidavit of discovery and declaring that he and Ryan had chartered the *Palestine* and had taken possession of Johnston for their sole benefit. This strange statement, so at variance with the facts, arrived three days before the papers filed by the four ostensible partners. How Parker expected to get away with this claim filed by Ryan since he had sold all but a one-sixteenth interest to the others, is not now easy to see.

The issue was further complicated by more double-crossing. Some Californians, including S. C. Allen, had heard of these islands and set out to persuade King Kamehameha IV and his ministers that Hawaii really owned them. They sent the *Kalima* to Hawaii where Allen secured the King's permission to hoist the Hawaiian flag on Johnston in June. Thus when the *Palestine* returned on July 22nd, they found the Pacific Guano Company markers overthrown and a strange flag flying. This they soon tore down, a house was built, some guano dug and two men left to hold the island until proper equipment could be installed.

In the meantime, Allen had persuaded the King to issue a proclamation announcing the annexation of Johnston by Hawaii on July 27th. Upon the strength of this, Allen sent Captain Borland in the *Gauntlet* to set up his rights. He found the two Pacific Company men there but they were not able to stop him from landing and prospecting. While the *Gauntlet* was riding at anchor, A. D. Piper, agent of the Pacific Company, arrived on the chartered ship *Radiant*, Captain Hallett, master. Piper had with him digging equipment and was expecting to start operations. He protested Borland's presence and in order to induce him to leave offered to charter his ship for the Pacific Company or to sell him a cargo at four dollars a ton. By this time, both Borland and Hallett agreed that no guano could be loaded, for there were no docks or facilities. The upshot was that both captains sailed away leaving Piper and eleven men in possession for the Pacific Company.

The Pacific Company now turned to diplomatic protest which was made through J. W. Borden, United States representative in Honolulu. He was able to report in January, 1859, that the Hawaiian king had withdrawn his claim. Attorney-General Black took up the conflicting affidavits and other papers submitted by Ryan and Parker opposing the Pacific Guano Company. In July he decided the Pacific Guano Company to be the rightful claimant to guano privileges. The corporation then could file its bond and December 9, 1859, the day after the Navassa certification, Lewis Cass proclaimed a like benefit to the Pacific Guano Company in the Johnston Islands. He thus announced to the world that the United States had assumed responsibility for interests in the broad Pacific. It was a fateful step.

Benson was beset by a second lot of competitors in the Pacific. C. A. Williams and Thomas Long, sailing for C. A. Williams and Company of New London, Connecticut, set out from Honolulu, January 19, 1859, to prospect for guano. They "discovered" it on three of the Phoenix Islands, McKean's, Phoenix and Birnie's. Also they made a similar find on Starve or Barren or Starbuck Island about twenty degrees east. Thomas Long at another time had a like experience on Enderbury Island of the Phoenix group. C. A. Williams and Company now formed the Phoenix Guano Company and supplied proofs and a bond. Cass in due time issued a proclamation on December 31, 1859, recognizing their rights on Starve, McKean's, Phoenix and Enderbury Islands.

Likewise caught in the same enthusiasm was a naval officer, Captain John M. Boothe of the U.S. Revenue Cutter, *Fenimore Cooper,* who reported he had discovered guano on

French Frigate Shoal, January 4, 1859, 23° 45′ N. Lat., 166° 25′ W. Long., near Hawaii. Secretary of the Navy Toucey duly reported it to the State Department and, shortly after, it was challenged by a private citizen who had likewise "discovered" it and felt grieved that a naval officer on government business should seek to enrich himself. No official action was taken and the claim was not recognized.

## IV

These later efforts were part and parcel of a new interest in Pacific guano stimulated in Europe. The use of Peruvian guano had been almost exclusive among European farmers because the product found in Polynesia was of different chemical composition. It did not have the ammonia content of the Peruvian variety and was therefore at first considered inferior. In 1858, however, the German chemist, Leibig, issued a statement to the effect that the phosphatic properties of the Pacific guanos were highly active fertilizing agents. This pronouncement gained currency in Europe and wakened official interest. American newspapers carried items in February, 1859, announcing that the French had taken over Clipperton Island, somewhat to the southwest of Mexico, and were going to work its guano.

All this interest and particularly the certificates issued in 1859 roused Benson to seek certification likewise and his move brought to official notice the difficulties which had been brewing between Benson and his associates in the guano business. Benson himself had been carrying on operations independently of the American Guano Company and had thus produced rivalry and schism. Benson had been developing private operations on a scale he wished to appear "colossal" and his activities had precipitated a "guano war." About the time that the first adverse reports on Baker Island and its alleged inaccessibility came in, namely in March, 1856, Benson had begun to build up a claim to another island, Howland, thirty-eight miles north of Baker and also to Malden and Arthur Islands 4° S. Lat. and 155° W. Long., near Starve Island. As usual, a sea captain was denominated "discoverer." Captain George E. Netcher of New Bedford had "discovered" these islands in 1842; Howland, which he had visited September 9, 1842, he had named after his lookout. Papers were prepared to show that in March, 1856, Netcher had made a discoverer's affidavit and had sold his "rights" to Benson, though a smudged date seems to indicate that the deed was really executed later and predated. Also it was made to appear that Benson had immediately transferred these rights to George W. Benson "for a valuable consideration." These papers were not turned over to the American Guano Company nor filed in the State Department in September, 1856, after the passage of the Guano Act.

When the American Guano Company sent out Arthur Benson to bring home a cargo of guano and to test the accessibility and value of Baker Island, he bore a private commission from his father which he was to execute though under pay of the company. He was to land on Howland and take possession of it like the others in the name of "Alfred G. Benson and associates," though in this case the "associates" were not the American Guano Company but two sea captains, the aforesaid Netcher and William W. Taylor of South Dartmouth, Massachusetts, of whom more later. This he did and when he returned, his father notified the State Department that he and Netcher had taken possession of Howland. About this time, on May 11, 1857, Benson bought from Captain John Stetson of New Haven his discoverer's rights to Christmas Island, 1° 58' N. Lat., 157° 10' W. Long. Two days later he transferred this island to George W. Benson in like manner as he had Howland and Malden, presumably the year previous. In fact, he was planning to have the American Guano Company buy these islands for his profit, as they had bought Baker and Jarvis. The only trouble was that his associates would not purchase, for they claimed that the rights to Howland's had been conveyed to the company by Turner and Benson in the early agreements and besides they thought they had enough islands.

Nothing daunted, Benson continued his independent operations. In April, 1858, he sent Captain Jason L. Pendleton to make formal occupation of Christmas Island, ostensibly owned by G. W. Benson, and of any other islands he might locate. The American Guano Company had every reason to expect him to try to work Howland Island which he claimed by right of his son's visit and Netcher's sale and this the company was going to prevent. In July, 1858, they sent Captain Theodore Lewis to take over Howland and in March, 1859, their agent at Baker, Charles H. Judd, visited the island and began the digging of guano. He also prospected for other islands and took possession of at least one, Palmyra, an atoll of 53 islets, 162° 11' W., 5° 49' N., 900 miles southwest of Hawaii, landing there October 19, 1859, from the Brig *Josephine*. Under these circumstances, Benson broke with Turner and withdrew from the Presidency of the company, October 13, 1858. Turner's attorney, Oscar Coles, was chosen to succeed him.

No sooner had Benson given up the direction of the original company than he became the prime mover in forming a rival. He now set up the United States Guano Company at his offices and put at its head Egbert Benson, a prominent

New York capitalist who was no kin of his. George W. Benson became its secretary. This company, incorporated November 25, 1858, planned to work Howland, Malden, Arthur and Christmas, and bought them of George W. Benson. Then it filed an elaborate dossier of papers with the State Department showing proofs of purchase and the condition of the guano and also including a bond for $100,000 for Howland Island. Like its competitor, the new company sold the right to take off guano to William H. Webb, associated with Edwin Croswell, and to the Boston firm of Glidden and Williams. After a year in office Egbert Benson withdrew and Alfred G. Benson became president of the company in December, 1859.

Benson and his half brother had not been content with these relatively small islands and had been preparing for expansion. During 1859, George W. Benson had been engaged in what were ostensibly private operations on his own hook. He had bought Washington, 4° 40′ N. Lat. and 160° 7′ W. Long., Starve or Starbuck, 5° 25′ S. Lat., 155° 56′ W. Long., and Gardner's 4° 40′ S. Lat., 174° 52′ W. Long., from various so-called "discoverers" and finally in February 7, 1859, he purchased from William W. Taylor, of Howland's fame, forty-two named islands or groups, some of which were in the Phoenix group already recognized as the property of the Phoenix Company. Most of them, however, were the so-called Line Islands north and south of Jarvis, and to the north and northeast of Samoa. George W. Benson filed claims for all of these in his own name at the State Department by April 28, 1859, which caused one of the officials of that office to describe it as a huge monopoly and an absurdity. Benson sold rights to Webb, Croswell, and Glidden and Williams to dig guano on his scattered possessions.

When Alfred G. Benson became president of the company, it purchased all of George W. Benson's accumulation.

The result was fantastic. At least nine of these islands or groups did not exist or were so carelessly located as to make it impossible to know what actual islands were meant. At least six of them were inhabited and not guano islands. Others were covered with gypsum or guano so adulterated by sand as to be useless. It was suspected that these guano promoters and their sea-captain friends had taken old charts and listed as many islands as they could imagine were possessed of guano and thus attempted to monopolize any possible wealth.

Alfred G. Benson filed bonds for these flocks of islands between December, 1859, and February, 1860, and received acknowledgments, which he seemed to deem sufficient recognition of his claims, dated March 2, 1860. Some guano was taken from them as before under the contracts with Webb and Crosswell and Glidden and Williams. The price of guano was going down and had reached forty dollars a ton.

Entrenched behind a formidable mound of documents, Benson determined to have it out with his erstwhile associates, and the United States Guano Company joined paper battle with the American Guano Company. This latter organization had been operating Howland's guano fields and making other "discoveries," such as Palmyra, and now Benson felt the time had come to stop it. He was determined to secure from the State Department a proclamation recognizing his rights to his great conglomeration, including Howland, such as had been issued to the operators of Navassa and to the Pacific and Phoenix Guano Companies. Both he and Glidden and Williams filed protests against including in the Phoenix Company's islands, Enderbury, which Benson claimed had been previously "discovered" by

Taylor. Also he submitted a new bond for Howland and pursued his demand so vigorously that in August while Cass was away, William Henry Trescott, his assistant secretary, signed a proclamation, August 8, 1860, recognizing the United States Guano Company as rightfully the operators of Howland Island.

This proclamation roused the American Guano Company to protest. Caleb S. Marshall, now its president, wrote Cass a vigorous letter and at the same time served notice on the United State Guano Company to keep off. To this notice, Alfred G. Benson replied by demanding a warship to aid his company in taking its own property, Howland.

Cass by this time was back and disturbed. Quite evidently the proclamation of Trescott was based on doubtful procedure. The American Guano Company was in possession of Howland and had been working it for over a year. The only claim the United States Guano Company had was that Arthur Benson had taken possession of it in the name of Alfred G. Benson and associates, meaning Netcher and Taylor, on an expedition for which he was paid by the American Guano Company. It was quite evident that Trescott had paid no attention to Black's rules laid down in 1857. Cass and Black went over the situation without arriving at any remedy. However, they did tighten up procedure and when H. J. Anderson acting as agent for the United States Guano Company with George W. Benson sought to get a similar proclamation regarding Christmas and Malden Island, Cass sent them Black's rules. These claimants must prove the existence of an estimated quantity of guano of proven good quality and must demonstrate continuous occupation and operation.

The American Guano Company now sought a proclamation for Baker and Jarvis and they were confronted by the same rules. Thereupon, they carefully made up a case with elaborate affidavits to prove their claim not only to Baker and Jarvis but also to Howland. These were submitted in the last days of Buchanan's Administration and one of the last things Black did as Secretary of State was to issue a proclamtion, March 2, 1861, recognizing the American Guano Company's right to Baker and Jarvis. No effort was made to revoke the action regarding Howland and in 1862 Benson climaxed his guano career by driving his competitors off of that island by force just as he had done at Enderbury in January, 1861. All during the trying days of the Civil War the offices of the State Department and the courts echoed with noise of this guano war. The American Guano Company could find no redress for Trescott's proclamation and both companies continued in competition during the next twenty years.

In this fashion the pursuit of guano had started the United States on the road to acquiring possessions not within the bounds of contiguous continental territory. Prominent Americans like Edward Bates were surprised to read in the papers that Governor Wilder and Governor Judd were ruling at Jarvis and Baker. Mr. Bates recorded in his diary, January 15, 1860, "The article says that these lone islands of the Pacific are now part and parcel of the American Republic. That is news to me. I never heard of those parts of the Republic before." New obligations had been assumed for isles in the oceans, and the first small beginnings of empire had been made at Navassa in the West Indies and on the coral reefs of the Pacific.

# 11. Pointing the Way to New Destiny in the Air Age

## I

THE apparent destiny of the United States to assume ever wider responsibility in a shrinking world was still being mapped in distant quarters of the earth's surface as the twentieth left the nineteenth century with History and proceeded to carve its own annals. Territorial acquisition of such areas as Alaska, Samoa, Hawaii, Puerto Rico and the Philippines left little popular attention for the guano dots where it had all started. But from time to time even in the last century, these islets served as indices of much larger activities than any they could stimulate or generate. They brought with them international and constitutional complications and finally it was upon them that some of the problems of World War II and the Air Age were framed in miniature.

The fruits of the feverish enterprise of the Bensons and their competitors in the guano industry involved the United States in international complications which were symptomatic of its growing responsibilities as a world power. American adventurers were none too learned in their international law nor too careful in their searches of title. Many of the dots they claimed to be uninhabited and unclaimed by other sovereignties, very soon appeared to have owners. The disputes which had arisen with Peru, with

Venezuela and with Haiti were but early examples of what was to follow.

On the eve of the Civil War these new complications began to appear. In 1859, the discovery of guano was claimed on Cayo Verde in the Bahama group and on Mona and Monita Islands in the Mona passage between Puerto Rico and Santo Domingo. Operations were started on these islands but British and Spanish authorities stopped them on charges of trespass and the United States acquiesced without protest. Shortly thereafter, Aves Island again came under diplomatic notice. The Atlantic and Pacific Guano Company of Fabens and Duff Green had found the island abandoned by the Philadelphia Company and had undertaken to work it. The Dutch now appeared and ordered them off. Such presumption aroused the Venezuelan government again and finally the Queen of Spain was called in to arbitrate. She decided in Venezuela's favor in 1865. The United States government, absorbed as it was by the Civil War, displayed no official concern in the fortunes of the Atlantic and Pacific Guano Company.

On the other hand, the Alta Vela case aroused much more interest and indeed became a *cause celèbre*. In 1860, a Baltimore firm, Patterson and Murguiondo, filed a discoverer's notice for another West Indian island, Alta Vela, 17° 28′ N. Lat., 71° 40′ W. Long. which the Cayo Verde operator likewise claimed. The Baltimore dealers began work only to be driven off almost immediately by the Santo Domingan government. Unfortunately, Patterson and Murguiondo had not completed the formalities under the Act of 1856, the Santo Domingan authorities hastened to grant guano concessions on the island to a New York firm, and the Civil War broke out. Secretary Seward and his successor, Hamilton Fish, ruled that the Baltimore firm had never complied with the act and that the United States would not intervene. The affair became involved in politics and despite years of vigorous effort, Patterson and Murguiondo could obtain no help from the United States government.

The last of these pre-Civil War claims in the West Indies to be challenged was the Grant and Wood operation on Sombrero since passed into the hands of Ross Wood and Son. In 1868, Great Britain took possession of this island as rightfully one of their Virgin Island group. Protest was made to Secretary Seward by the American operators but despite the fact that the island had been included in an official list of guano islands published the year before, the Department would take no action as Seward could find no record that "the title of citizens of the United States to the guano on that island was ever recognized by the President."

Almost immediately, further controversies were stirred up by the activities of a new promoter. James W. Jennett started a quest for guano shortly after the close of the Civil War and wherever he began operations there was generally diplomatic controversy. As the Bensons had scoured the Pacific, so Jennett explored the Caribbean. He made it a profession. In 1868 he filed notice of the discovery of guano on Serrano off Nicaragua and the next year on Quita Sueño and Roncador in the same locality and on Pedro and Petrel near Jamaica. The necessary formalities were completed and acknowledged by the State Department and Jennett disappears for ten years. Then between 1879 and 1884 he filed another batch, which he swore he had visited in the Sixties. These were mostly off the coast of Mexico. Eight of the operations were duly bonded and listed and as before, Jennett assigned his interests as soon as they were recognized. Unfortunately Jennett was careless about his facts. Most of his claims brought diplomatic protests from

Honduras, Nicaragua, Mexico, Colombia and Great Britain. The protests of Britain and Mexico were reasonable in the State Department's eyes and orders were issued to strike some of the islands off the list.

During the years after the Civil War various inroads were made upon the Pacific guano empire. The American and United States Guano Companies continued to be active into the Seventies, still under the direction of A. G. Benson. The business of these operators was limited by the dwindling supply of guano and the extension of British interest. Benson in 1868 reported that Englishmen were on Malden and asked unsuccessfully for a warship to protect the rights of his company.

Real British activity did not begin until the late Eighties and was probably stimulated by the possibility of the growing ambitions of at least one other power, notably Germany. Then Great Britain started taking over these islands, particularly as she found most of them abandoned by the United States guano diggers. In 1888 England occupied Christmas Island and the Washington-Fanning group; on this latter location a cable station was established. In 1889 she took possession of Jarvis and Palmyra and in 1892 of Johnston Island and the Phoenix group including Canton and Enderbury. Most of these islands were leased to English and Australian guano firms, principally to the Pacific Islands Company. In all these the United States displayed little interest. Fertilizer styles were changing, nitrates were more desired than guano. At that time the United States attached no strategic value to them and contented itself with a portion of the Samoan Islands. Howland and Baker were the only islands left to the nation by mapmakers. All the "great monopoly" of the United States was labeled "British Polynesia."

Of greater significance in the light of Pearl Harbor was the dispute between the United States and Japan resulting from the last attempt of our citizens to invoke the Act of 1856. Andrew A. Rosehill filed some papers at the State Department in 1889 to prove that he had discovered guano and had taken possession of Marcus Island, 24° 14' N. Lat., 154° E. Long. This island near the Bonin group was much closer to Japan than the other guano dots. The State Department instructed him as to what further steps he must take and meanwhile he had built a small house there and left a man and his wife to maintain possession. He was delayed in returning and the lonesome couple took advantage of a passing ship to abandon their post. Though Rosehill revisited the island finally in 1895 and 1896 he was still without necessary capital to work the deposits. At length, in 1898, Japan notified the United States that the island was hers.

Despite this notification Rosehill finally succeeded in 1902 in getting money for his project and sought to complete formalities by filing a bond. The State Department was reluctant to interfere with what had become a Japanese guano business and Rosehill sought political aid. Congressman George C. Perkins urged his case with the Secretary but he was unsuccessful. The Department announced finally "the claims of Captain Rosehill remain in abeyance awaiting direct settlement between the governments of the United States and Japan." Maps of the early twentieth century marked the island as belonging to the United States but the Japanese had actual possession.

In short, the United States government had never thought these guano reefs worth a controversy, particularly as new types of fertilizers made guano less and less important. The

State Department paid little attention to alleged encroachments.

## II

These islands raised constitutional as well as diplomatic questions. For many years any definition of the nature of the sovereignty and responsibilities of the United States, if any, was neatly side-stepped. The original act made use of a curious phrase when it declared that after the necessary formalities had been complied with, the guano islands "shall be considered as appertaining to the United States" though it was further stated that nothing in the act "shall be construed as obliging the United States to retain possession" of the islands after the guano had been removed. Provision was made for government and a rule of law by extending the statutes applying to "all acts done and offenses or crimes committed . . . on the high seas on board a merchant ship or vessel belonging to the United States." The constitutionality of this procedure was not tested for many years but finally it was questioned late in the nineteenth century and the Supreme Court was thereby given an opportunity to speak.

There was murder done on Navassa in 1889 when Negro laborers attacked their white bosses and killed several men. At the request of the American consul at Kingston, Jamaica, a British warship was sent to the island to maintain order and the U.S.S. *Kearsarge* brought the Negroes to Baltimore for trial. Upon their conviction under the act of 1856, their counsel took an appeal to the Supreme Court on the grounds the act was unconstitutional and that the United States District Court at Baltimore had no jurisdiction over crimes committed on Navassa which was not part of the United States. The Supreme Court denied the appeal and decided that the island of Navassa "must be considered as appertaining to the United States." "Appertaining" was still the curious word used.

In 1904 a State Department official summed it up as follows: "The United States possesses no sovereign or territorial rights over guano islands. It simply protects American citizens who discover guano on an island, or their assigns, in the prosecution of their enterprise which extends only to appropriation and disposal of guano.

"The guano acts extend to guano islands only such laws of the United States as relate to merchant ships and vessels, and offenses committed on the high seas."

This statement so pleased Assistant Secretary Adee that he endorsed it: "It is a convenient formula for future use. Note in your *Index Rerum.*"

Problems of navigation connected with the new shipping routes made possible by the construction of the Panama Canal raised anew this question of sovereignty. Navassa now was in a direct sea lane from New York to Panama and was the first landfall sighted by ships sailing northward from the Canal. Its position made it a menace and a lighthouse was deemed necessary to mark its position and warn shipping. By this time guano digging had ceased, the operating company had failed, and the island was abandoned .

General George W. Gordon, Representative from Tennessee, introduced a bill to erect a lighthouse to serve as a monument to Matthew Fontaine Maury; it was proposed to build this structure on Navassa. In due course, a congressional committee stopped to view Navassa and Representative Esch was moved to poetical expression. One of his stanzas expressed his hope:

> Soon may thy reign of terror end
> And welcome lights their rays extend

To gladden the weary storm-tossed sailor's sight
On ships that pass by in the night—Navassa.

The proposal to commemorate Maury's services was abandoned after Gordon's death but Congress provided the light. The House, under the influence of a reading of Esch's poetic plea by Adamson of Georgia, inserted the necessary appropriation and the Senate concurred. The purpose of Congress thus to light more adequately an important approach to the Panama Canal made necessary a public notice to the world. President Wilson proclaimed on January 17, 1916, that whereas the Island of Navassa was then "not under the sole and exclusive jurisdiction of any other government," and whereas Congress had decided to build a light station thereon, "the said Island of Navassa in the West Indies be and the same is hereby reserved for lighthouse purposes, such reservation being deemed necessary in the public interests, subject to such legislative action as the Congress of the United States may take with respect thereto."

During the First World War, attention was turned for strategic reasons to other of the guano islands such as Serrano, Quita Sueño, Roncador Cay and the Swan Islands. These latter were in the hands of a Swan Island Company who were growing cocoanuts on them and the United Fruit Company had erected a wireless station thereon. The war stimulated interest and Assistant Secretary Franklin D. Roosevelt recommended that they be taken over for the use of the navy. The end of the war came not long after this and no formal action was taken regarding the Swan Islands. However, Serrano and Quita Sueño were held by Proclamation of February 25, 1919, to be under the sole and exclusive jurisdiction of the United States, although later upon the protest of Colombia, the nationals of the latter were accorded some rights by agreement of April 10, 1928. Roncador was made a lighthouse reservation on June 5, 1919, and declared to be under the sole and exclusive jurisdiction of the United States. The question of sovereignty had advanced no nearer an official answer than in the case of Navassa.

Not until the Coolidge Administration was the final clarification made. Attorney General John G. Sargent on June 24, 1925, issued an opinion "that the dominion of the United States was extended over the Swan Islands by the President, as evidenced by the certificate of Secretary Seward, dated February 11, 1863, and that the sovereignty of the United States attached to said islands as of that date." The question was thus finally settled after seventy years of official uncertainty. These islands were possessions. The government thereupon erected radio and meteorological stations upon them and refused to accept Honduran protests.

### III

The advent of the Air Age and the coming of transpacific air traffic together with the increasing realization of the strategic implications of air and naval bases as World War II approached, caused the United States to resume interest in these guano islands for reasons other than their fertilizing or lighthouse possibilities. In the 1930's, airways were marked, clippers were flown from the United States to China and from Canada to Australia. These passenger services called for alighting and fueling stations which might also have defense uses and these might be placed on guano islands, mostly long-since abandoned. Once more the United States government became aware of Johnston, of Canton, of Enderbury, of Christmas, of Jarvis, Howland and Baker.

In 1928, the pioneer aviator, Kingsford-Smith, flew the *Southern Cross* from San Francisco to Sydney, Australia.

He was an advance agent whose coming foretold the creation of regular service flights. There was need of a station midway between Hawaii and New Zealand and here were myriads of islands. Active imaginations began to take hold of the problem. Then the determination in 1934 to free the Philippines made the United States more defense conscious and late in that year the President made a new disposition of some of the guano islands in the interest of defense. Johnston Island had been claimed by Great Britain and as early as 1892 she had announced an intention to build a cable station there. The strong protest of Hawaii may have deterred her for she did not make installation on either Johnston or Palmyra. In 1926, President Coolidge had felt free to turn over Johnston to the Department of Agriculture for a bird refuge and breeding ground. But in 1934, there seemed more significant use at hand. On December 29th, President Roosevelt assigned Johnston Island and Kingman Reef to the Navy Department together with Wake and Sand Islands. Johnston straightway became a naval base.

Air travel combined with national defense to urge government attention to other guano islands. The State Department began negotiations with the British Foreign Office on the question of who owned the scattered dots to which each nation had some historic claim. These negotiations were extremely leisurely and in the meantime, Mr. Jay Pierrepont Moffat, in charge of the State Department desk dealing with these islands, understood that both nations had agreed that neither would move in this area until these complex questions of ownership were finally settled.

The Department of Commerce, likewise, became interested in aiding Pan American Airways Incorporated, then the only American line operating in that part of the world, to find the air stations it needed in order to project pas-

senger routes to Australia. Attention was naturally directed
to our oldest possessions where our claims were least challenged, namely Baker, Howland and Jarvis. It was at first
thought that those islands might supply at least one landing field for land based planes. Under the direction of the
Secretary of Commerce, William T. Miller, Superintendent
of Airways of the Bureau of Air Commerce, was despatched
as one of the latest advance agents of American interest.
Sailing on the U.S. Coast Guard *Itasca,* he reached Jarvis
and there landed on March 26, 1935. Here the American
flag was raised and a small party of colonists set out to create the little post of Millersville in honor of the leader. Four
days later the ceremony was repeated on Howland and on
April 3, the *Itasca* reached Baker. Here another outpost
was established, named Meyerton after Captain H. A.
Meyer, U.S.A., who was in charge of laying out the camps
on these islands. The American flag was back on the Equator.

The next year, these colonists were withdrawn temporarily
while a change of administration was in process. President
Roosevelt issued an executive order, May 13, 1936, placing
these islands under the jurisdiction of the Department of
the Interior. There they were to be the responsibility of the
relatively new Division of Territories and Island Possessions
created in June, 1934 and administered by Dr. Ernest
Gruening, its first director, a New York City author and
newspaper man, a Harvard graduate who had taken an
M.D. but had turned to journalism, editing first the *Nation,*
and then the Portland (Me.) *Evening News,* and the *New
York Evening Post.* He had distinguished himself in the
field of international relations by writing a standard work,
*Mexico and its Heritage.*

Dr. Gruening chose as his field representative, Richard

Blackburn Black, an experienced engineer of proved administrative ability. He had graduated in civil engineering at the University of North Dakota in 1926. Since then, he had been engaged in railroad building and mine safety operations. Also, he had gone to Antarctica with Byrd, 1933–35, where he had won the Admiral's high praise. Mr. Black was now to set up a field office for the Division in Honolulu and on July 8, 1936, he established himself in the Iolani Palace. He was to reestablish American interest on Jarvis, Baker and Howland.

Lighthouses and weather stations were to be maintained there, each in charge of four students from the Kamehameha Boys School of Honolulu. These boys would do short tours of duty and then be relieved. Black was to organize a series of cruises which at regular intervals would visit the stations bringing supplies and replacements. In this way, the observations could be continued with due precaution against too prolonged exposuse to the monotony of so isolated an existence. In the spring of 1937, an airstrip was built on Howland under the direction of Robert Leslie Campbell, Divisional Airport Inspector for the Department of Commerce with the help of the Army, the Navy, the W.P.A. and the Department of Interior. However, it was not long before it became apparent that these islands would not do. It was no easier to land upon them than it had been in the 1850's. There were neither harbors nor anchorages. The Naval vessels bringing supplies would have to lie far off shore while landing parties made hazardous ventures over the reefs and through the surf. Furthermore, Pan-Am was using sea planes and these islands could serve only land based planes.

But seeking other bases raised the diplomatic complications which had been in the background for so long. His Majesty's Government, not unmindful of American activity on Baker, Howland and Jarvis, had been refurbishing its own claims. H.M.S. *Leith* was sent on a tour of duty. This war vessel had visited Christmas Island in February, 1937, to land radio equipment, had inspected the Phoenix Islands and had looked in upon the Americans at Jarvis. In the meantime, the British had published an Order in Council dated March 18, 1937, annexing the Phoenix Islands, which included Canton and Enderbury, to the Gilbert and Ellice Islands Colony.

The existence of rival claims to these "line islands" was brought into sharper focus by an affair of the heavens. A total eclipse of the sun was scheduled for June which could best be seen on Canton. The astronomers of England and the United States organized expeditions and at the appointed time two warships, the U.S.S. *Avocet* and H.M.S. *Wellington* landed scientists. While the navy officers reflected the rivalry, these men of learning had no difficulty in fraternizing and pursuing their investigations without any "international incidents." Later in the year, the *Leith* again visited Canton and set up a radio station just as she had upon Christmas Island.

The matter of ownership of these isles was increasing in importance as the plans of air transport were further advanced. Pan-Am had continued to explore the routes between the United States and Asia and Australia. One of their clippers had made a first flight between Hawaii and New Zealand in March, 1937. They first planned to use Kingman Reef as a convenient half-way stopping point between Hawaii and Samoa and had anchored a schooner, *The Trade Wind,* there to serve as a supply ship and hostel. Dr. Gruening, in the meantime, had been receiving reports of the shortcomings of the arrangements available for air stations on Baker, Jarvis, Howland and Kingman, so he decided to go out and direct a search for new and better facilities. He consulted the State Department and secured from them their cooperation in his project and their list of the various islands, the ownership of which was being discussed by the United States and Great Britain.

Dr. Gruening went to Honolulu in October, 1937, and there completed plans for his voyage of inspection on the Coast Guard Cutter, *Taney.* His first stop was at Palmyra, then politically a part of the distant City and County of Honolulu. Then he proceeded to Washington, Fanning and Christmas Island. On the latter, he found some twenty-five Tahitian families growing cocoanuts under a concession which the British had granted in the form of a lease in the 1890's to a French priest from Tahiti. These Polynesians were directed by a French manager who was living there with his wife and son and a Czechoslovak assistant. British authority was represented by a British Administrator. This level island of hard-packed coral, thirty miles long with a lagoon suitable for sea plane alighting seemed to Dr. Gruening ideal for the purpose.

From thence, the *Taney* sailed to Howland, Baker and Jarvis and on to the Phoenix group where five islands were inspected including Canton and Enderbury. Here Dr. Gruening made an unwelcome and unexpected discovery. Nailed to some palm trees on these Phoenix islands were proclamations declaring these islands, most of which were uninhabited, to be part of the Gilbert and Ellice Administration of His Britannic Majesty's domain.

On Canton Island, he found the radio station in charge of two British operators. This island, like Christmas, Dr. Gruening concluded, was suitable for an air station for either land or sea-based planes. He concluded his tour with visits at Kingman Reef and the Samoan Islands.

The result of this cruise was the conviction that Jarvis, Baker, Howland, Kingman Reef and Samoa were unsuitable for air service stations and this judgment was in part confirmed by a serious plane accident at Kingman Reef in January, 1938, which convinced Pan-Am that new arrangements must be made. Dr. Gruening thereupon recommended to President Roosevelt and Mr. Moffatt at the State Department that the United States establish itself at Christmas and Canton. The State Department felt that the claim to Christmas had been forfeited because no protest had been made against the Tahiti cocoanut growers these many years, so the decision was taken to proceed on Canton.

To this end, Dr. Gruening directed Richard B. Black on February 16, 1938, to establish American interests on Canton and Enderbury and the cutter *Taney* set off with complete secrecy for this purpose under the authority of an Executive Order which the President was to issue on March 3rd. On March 6th, Mr. Black raised the United States flag on Enderbury and then proceeded on the next day to Canton. Here he was met by Geoffrey V. Langdale and Thomas Manning, British residents, supported by their Fiji houseboy. They objected officially to the raising of the American flag. Despite this protest, Black erected a temporary pole 100 yards from the British and up went the Stars and Stripes. Seven men were left to set up a radio station. On April 1st, Secretary Ickes licensed Pan-Am to use Canton and in May the U.S.S. *Ontario* arrived with airline representatives to plan the seaplanes base.

In the meantime, guano diplomatic negotiations took on unwonted vigor. The British filed emphatic objections. The State Department, in return, pointed out that the British had violated the understanding by their occupation of Canton and by the proclamation of title to the Phoenix Islands.

It pointed out the needs of air transportation and indicated that Britain might have the use of any American facilities constructed upon payment of reasonable fees. Besides, Britain had so many, many islands while the United States possessed none suitable for the purpose.

The British countered by explaining they planned to relieve overcrowded conditions on the Gilbert and Ellice Islands by bringing two hundred of the natives to grow cocoanuts on Canton. The island, to be sure, was then barren and cocoanut trees could not bear for seven years. But Britain was going to feed the colonists on rice until the harvest came at long last. This rice would then be paid for by the cocoanuts. However, after sufficient of this interchange, on August 10, 1938, the United States and Great Britain agreed to the common use by the two nations of Canton and Enderbury. The details were worked out in an exchange of notes which took place on April 6, 1939. For fifty years, the United States and Great Britain were to enjoy joint use without raising the question of ownership. A week later, the United States entered into a contract with Pan-Am, whereby they obtained leases to certain portions of Canton. They constructed the necessary buildings and installations and in August, on their first flight, a great Boeing Clipper with seventy-two passengers made a stop at the new station.

The United States had not been unmindful of the defense aspect of these new air interests. A naval seaplane base had been built on Johnston and now another was constructed on Palmyra in the first months of World War II, 1939–1940. No sooner had the disaster at Pearl Harbor brought the United States into the conflict than these small islets began to bear some of its brunt. Only a few days elapsed before news came of Japanese aggression upon these islands. The

United States naval outpost, Johnston Island, was shelled. Attacks were likewise made on Palmyra, Canton, Baker and Howland. On December 8th and 10th, Japanese war vessels shelled Baker and Howland, where the usual quota of aereological observers was stationed. On Howland, two of the four were killed. Aid was sent but not until January 31st could a destroyer reach them. On Howland they found the two survivors, hungry and almost naked. They took them on board and then proceeded to Baker. Here as of yore, there was difficulty, the surf was running high and landing was impossible. With great difficulty, the four men were brought off on a frail surf boat which smashed in the shark-infested waters. But their rescue was accomplished and the survivors taken to Honolulu. Soon there was a return raid. In March, the American press bore the headlines, "U.S. Navy Raids Marcus Island." The Japanese had established an air base thereon which was the object of the attack and which they maintained throughout the war.

Japan soon turned her attention to Canton. At the beginning of World War II, Robert L. Campbell was on that island directing a large construction crew. These were soon evacuated to Samoa in anticipation of a Japanese air attack. This eventually occurred and most of this installation was destroyed. However, the facilities were rebuilt and extensive use was made of them during the conflict. The Japanese also destroyed the airstrip on Howland and the United States Navy demolished American installations on Jarvis to prevent their use by the Japanese. Here again the United States returned in the course of the war and in 1943 the army moved into Baker and built a Marston Mat air strip. Bases were also constructed on the British isles of Christmas and Funafuti, the latter in the Union group.

With the coming of peace, there was immediate concern

for the two principal objectives of the renewed interest in the Pacific, defense and commercial aviation. The main problem was the question between the United States and Great Britain combined with the related question of what was to be the disposition of the islands which Japan either owned or held under mandate, i.e., the Bonins and the old German possessions. The United States continued to occupy the Japanese-owned Bonin islands including the guano island, Marcus, and entered into negotiation with Great Britain about the others. At first the military, naval and air forces were earnest that the United States build up a great rim of outer defenses in Polynesia. It was hoped that as part of the new understanding with Great Britain which included a large loan to our ally, we could receive a large share of islands then under British or New Zealand mandate or ownership, including the Phoenix Islands and others in the Union and Cook groups in the vicinity of Samoa.

Diplomatic conversations were held and there was debate in Congress. Some of the more earnest wanted this readjustment of ownership in the Pacific completed before the British loan was approved and to include acknowledgment of our long standing claim to the Phoenix Islands and to Christmas. However, Great Britain was not so minded and as time passed, it became apparent that the improvement of jet airplanes was making the island bases of less importance. So in the end, little was changed. American ownership is acknowledged at Johnston, Sand and Palmyra in the Hawaiian radius and at Baker, Howland and Jarvis on the Line. The United States still maintains a claim to certain other of the so-called Line Islands, Caroline, Christmas, Flint, Malden, Starbuck and Vostok, as well as to the Northern Cook Islands, the Phoenix Islands and the Union Islands. Most of these claims arise from the early guano interest. The United States, has, in addition, inaugurated a successful association with Great Britain on Canton Island which is now a humming air travel station. Two little settlements have developed, Northside and Southside, American and British. At Northside is the airport and Southside the residential section. A school has been set up and a hotel and a fire department. A British Administrator and an American Administrator share responsibility, and two post-offices, British and American, are maintained. The American representative is responsible to three departments. As United States Resident Administrator, he reports to the Department of the Interior, as Island Manager for Civil Aeronautics Administration, he is connected with the Department of Commerce and as United States Deputy Marshal, he is under the Department of Justice. The Americans, manning the airways, have recreated a Polynesian interest for the United States, as man himself, or his voice, travels everywhere on the wings of the wind and over the waves of the ether.

Gruening, Miller, Black and Campbell are among those of but the latest generation of the many who over the hundred and eighty years of our national existence have met the challenges of succeeding epochs and have carried American interests out into ever more distant and unknown regions. They, like their predecessors, have made paths for others to follow in the continuing acceptance of that greater responsibility which is sometimes described as American destiny.

# Appendix I
## First Agents and Consular Appointments

The need for supplies caused the American Continental Congress to employ agents for trading purposes. In June, 1776, the Committee on Secret Correspondence sent its secretary, William Bingham, to St. Pierre on the French Island of Martinique and later Samuel Parsons functioned there in like capacity. At Cap François and the Mole St. Nicholas on the island of Haiti, Stephen Ceronio and John Duprey had a similar assignment. Even more important was the agency at the Dutch island of St. Eustatius where a vital supply depot was operated by Samuel Curzon while his partner, Isaac Gouverneur, was in charge at Curaçao. The new states likewise sent agents to purchase supplies. Abraham Van Bibber represented Maryland at Martinique where he and his partner, Richard Harrison, sought to care for Virginia's interests at well.

On November 4, 1780, William Palfrey, recently paymaster general of the army, was elected consul to be stationed in France. Next June, Congress elected Robert Smith agent at Havana; it made Thomas Barclay vice consul in France and in October he succeeded Palfrey to full power. In 1783, John Marsden Pintard was elected consul at Madeira and in 1786 Samuel Shaw and Thomas Randal were chosen consul and vice consul at Canton, China. This was the extent of Congressional appointment and it may be noted that no consuls were created for ports on the Western Hemisphere.

During the decade before the adoption of the Constitution, Congress occasionally debated the creation of a consular system but the sole definite result was a resolution that only American citizens might serve as consuls and the negotiation of a separate consular convention with France after seemingly interminable argument and disputing regarding terms. After eight years of discussion the treaty was signed November 14, 1788. The new Senate ratified it and it was proclaimed in effect April 9, 1790.

Jacob Mayer of Pennsylvania was sent to Cap François in 1796 and next year Frederick Folger of Maryland was commissioned to Aux Cayes. James Yard had been sent to Santa Cruz in the Danish West

221

Indies in 1791 and David M. Clarkson and Benjamin H. P. Phillips in 1793 to the Dutch possessions at St. Eustatius and Curaçao. All these were from Pennsylvania. The only agent tried to British territory was Samuel Cooper Johonnet of Massachusetts, in 1793, at Demarara in British Guiana. However, the British began serious privateering depredations in 1793 for which the Jay treaty provided damages. It was then necessary to collect evidence of these captures, so in 1794 and in the year that followed, a series of agents were sent down or commissioned to gather testimony; these included N. C. Higginson, James and William Perot, Silas Talbot, John Trumbull, Henry Cray and William Savage. These occasionally sought to care for stranded mariners and arrange for the release of others who might be held in durance vile.

# Appendix II

## Some Notes on Spanish West Indian Trade with the United States

From September 1789 to September 1790, exports from the United States to the Spanish West Indies were valued at about $100,000; fifty per cent was flour. Cuba had to buy seventy-five per cent of its flour outside the Spanish empire. Spain required that this large quantity be bought from Spanish merchants and pass through the European ports of Spain, thus increasing the cost by the various profits, commissions, freight charges and taxes collected by the Spanish government and merchants. Flour that sold for five or six dollars in the United States, cost from ten to sixteen dollars a barrel in Cuba. Imports were correspondingly slight, the largest item being a half-million pounds of sugar.

On June 9, 1793, the ports of New Orleans, Pensacola and St. Augustine had been opened to countries with which Spain had treaties if the vessels touched first at a Spanish port. In spite of United States disqualification, contraband trade flourished.

The first Spanish consuls, Jaudenes and Viar, and their agents were instructed to collect information in regard to possible separatist intrigues in the western part of the United States. The Spanish consuls at Boston and New York were John and Thomas Stoughton and as John Stoughton was Jaudenes's father-in-law, it was all a nice family affair.

The concessions given these men were fought by Spanish merchants, especially those who had enjoyed a monopoly of the colonial trade in peace-time, so a partial suspension had been ordered in 1794, but no appreciable obedience was observed. Jaudenes in particular was under fire. Many Cubans protested his high charges for permits and the resulting high prices charged them for goods. Pickering, the Secretary of State, complained of his plotting with disaffected Americans in the Mississippi Valley. The Spanish government soon gave him another place which was looked upon as a promotion.

In 1790–1791 (September to September) exports to the Spanish West Indies were reported as valued at $65,222.29, there was some increase by 1792–1793 to $159,426 but the effect of the relaxation of restriction is seen when the figures for the next three years are noted. Exports for 1793–1794, 1794–1795, 1795–1796, were valued at $872,616, $1,389,219, and $1,821,347, respectively. The latter figure would have been greater undoubtedly had not trade been cut off in the last three months. There are no total figures for imports, but if sugar is taken for an index the 1,067,987 lbs. imported in 1790–1791 became 4,651,714 lbs. in 1794–1795 only to decrease to 3,961,576 in 1795–1796. In 1790 (calendar, not fiscal year as in above), Philadelphia Custom House records show no vessels clearing for Havana and five entering from there. There are no further clearance records surviving until 1802 but the entries tell the story. In 1793, there were nine entries from Havana, in 1794, forty-one, in 1795, thirty-four (one from Santiago), and in 1796, thirty-five (one from Nuevitas and four from Santiago).

As soon as Yrujo heard of the outbreak of war, he induced a captain to hurry the news to Cuba by permitting him to sell 500 barrels of flour there; and shortly thereafter, he gave James Barry a permit to introduce 20,000 barrels. Puerto Rico had sent for food but as Yrujo had no funds with which to procure it, he got Barry to supply Puerto Rico on credit in return for this permission to sell to Cuba. Godoy rebuked Yrujo but gave grudging permission. Yrujo complained particularly against Yznardi. He claimed that the latter's advertisements sent the price of flour up and notified British cruisers to lie in wait for the food ships as they left the United States.

Exports in 1796–1797 amounted in value to $2,879,170 and in 1797–1798, to $5,298,659. Imports (using sugar as an example) for the two years respectively, amounted to 20,947,249 and 40,202,868 lbs. The entries into Philadelphia for the calendar year 1798 were forty-eight from Cuba, two from Puerto Rico, while for the first time a significant item appears, five ships from the port of La Guaira in Venezuela. 1798 shows fifty-eight ships from Cuba, four from Puerto Rico and nine from La Guaira. The Spanish-American empire was buying not only flour and other provisions but spirits and wine, lumber and iron, shoes, hats, dry goods, and furniture. The United States bought principally sugar, molasses, brandy and rum, coffee, cocoa, indigo, tobacco, and cigars.

Exports for 1797–1798 and 1800–1801 were valued at $5,298,659 and $9,070,022, respectively; and sugar imports for the same periods amounted to 40,202,868 and 74,514,618 lbs. respectively. Considerable items are first listed in this period as to and from South America. Exports to this region amounted to $532,153 in 1800–1801 and the largest listed item of import was 2,131,137 lbs. of cocoa. The Philadelphia statistics show that the fifty-eight ships from Cuba in 1798 had been increased to ninety-eight in 1801, the four from Puerto Rico had become six and the nine from Venezuela had become fourteen; in addition, five were listed from the La Plata in 1801. In 1798, the total from the Spanish-American empire had been seventy-five and in 1801 this had become 137.

Exports for 1800–1801, 1801–1802, and 1802–1803 were valued at $9,070,022, $6,047,688, and $938,289 respectively, and sugar import for the same periods amounted to 74,514,618, 15,106,283, and 8,051,882 lbs. respectively. Entries to Philadelphia from Cuba dropped from ninety-eight in 1801 to twenty in 1803, Puerto Rico entries disappeared, and the Venezuelan entries dropped from fourteen to three.

Trade reached its high point in 1806–1807 when exports amounted to $13,025,579 and the importation of sugar 87,763,464 lbs. The calendar year 1807 brought 200 vessels from Spanish America to Philadelphia, 138 from Cuba, eighteen from Puerto Rico, twenty-nine from Venezuela, but two from the La Plata and seven from Vera Cruz. One hundred and seventy-seven ships cleared from Philadelphia for Spanish-America, one hundred and fifteen for Cuba, five for Puerto Rico, ten for Venezuela, one for the La Plata and three for Vera Cruz. The La Plata authorities were not friendly and those in Venezuela sometimes had temperament.

Exports dropped from $13,025,579 in 1806–1807 to $6,685,617 in 1808–1809 and sugar imports from 87,763,464 lbs. in 1806–1807 to 34,657,330 lbs. in 1808–1809. According to the Philadelphia statistics the drop in the number of vessels was not so marked. The calendar year 1809 showed a decrease of entries of from 200 in 1807 to 184 and of clearances from 177 to 126; Cuban entries of 138 became ninety-one, Puerto Rican *increased* eighteen to thirty, and Venezuelan, twenty-nine to thirty. Cuban clearances declined from 115 to eighty, Puerto Rican increased from five to twenty-six, Venezuelan increased from ten to fifteen.

During these uncertain years, even when trade was open, it was burdened by the most puzzling customs impositions. The most vigorous of United States agents, Henry Hill, Jr., was indefatigable in his efforts to discover how these duties were calculated. The problem is best understood by an examination of a report he made dated November 1-10, 1805. Nothing much more formidable can be imagined and the procedure well illustrates differences between Spanish and American methods.

"1. A duty of 32½ pr Ct on all articles imported in American vessels is exacted on a valuation which reduces it to an average of about 26 pr Ct on the Invoice cost and charges in the United States—except on flour, which pays 1 25/100 Dollars besides the 32½ pr Ct., and is a favor to the Count de Morpox, in consideration of the suspension of a permission granted him by royal authority previous to the present war for the exclusive introduction of that article; which enhances the duty on flour to [$] 4 40/100 pr Bbl—an article of the first necessity, of which at least 70,000 bbls are annually required for the consumption of the population of Havana and its vicinity alone.

2d. A duty of 32½ pr Ct is exacted on the sale of every American Vessel, (unless to a Spanish subject and incorporated in the Spanish marine) whether such sale is voluntary or caused from necessity—of which there are three examples now in this port of Vessels condemned as unfit for sea.

3d. Captains of Vessels before they are allowed to land or have any communication from shore, are required to produce their manifests to the boarding officer of the Custom House. Another is required to be presented by the consignee, and each consignee of Cargo is obliged to produce his separate Invoice—This is well enough, in order to prevent frauds being committed on the revenue—But, they must all undergo a translation by a person placed there for that purpose, whose charge is exhorbitant and is paid by the American merchant, and is an imposition which robs our commerce of at least 15,000 Dollars annually— It is totally unnecessary, for each consignee might translate his own Invoice without expence [*sic*] or delay, which would leave no opening for a fraud on the revenue, and is an imposition imposed for the express purpose of favoring the person who holds this lucrative place.

4th. Some alteration having taken place on the 28th of May last in the regulation of duty, which was published officially, it was expressly allowed by the 5th article of that regulation, that neutral vessels importing goods of the growth or manufacture of Spain, with certificates from the Custom Houses whence they should be cleared in Spain, of their being such, should pay no more duty on such goods than is exacted when imported in Spanish Vessels. Goods of this description have been since imported in American Vessels, with all the proofs of their origin required by P[ort] regulations and have been denied the priviledge [*sic*] conceded by it; under the pretext that such goods must be the property of Spanish subjects.

5. By order of the Intendant of the 28th of June last, Vessels from neutral ports are required to have certificates from the Spanish Consuls there, if any, if not, from persons authorized to grant them by the Spanish Ambassador, to each particular Invoice, certifying the port to which the Vessel is destined, to the weight, measure, quality, quantity, and value of the goods they contain—which certificates are not asked for here at the Custom House, but may be demanded, and in default of them, the vessel be subjected to detention, and the goods to confiscation. This absurd and unnecessary imposition, I have good reasons to believe was imposed at the particular instance & request of the Spanish Consuls in the United States.

6th If by mistake or ignorance more goods are entered than are on board, the duty notwithstanding is exacted upon the quantity entered. If, from the same cause less are entered than are found on board, the remainder are confiscated without any indulgence. And although an article of weight or measure may have lost before delivery near the whole of its original quantity, the duty is exacted on the quantity expressed in the Invoice.

7th All goods are obliged to be passed through the Custom House, and if dry, articles are taken out of their several packages for examination, are frequently plundered, and sometimes detained several months, unless gratifications are given to obtain their release.

8th Masters of Vessels on their arrival are obliged to present themselves to the Captain of the port, and subscribe to his regulations, and if they deviate the least from this, or from any other cause are so unfortunate as to offend this petulent [*sic*], petty despot of the Harbour, are frequently thrown into a prison the most loathsome in the world, among criminals of every class of crime, and description of colour, or placed in the public stocks exposed to public view and ridicule, untill he is pleased to liberate them.

9th Vessels clearing from the United States for the Island of Cuba *generally*, meet with imposition and detention from that cause. The port to which they are bound is required to be designated in their papers.

10th There is no remission of duty on reexportation of any article, and an exportation duty of 9½ pr Ct is exacted. Thus, the person importing goods here, after they are once landed, is obliged to sell them at any price he can obtain; for loaded with such heavy impositions, there is no market to which he can send them, with a prospect of bettering himself.

11th  Vessels putting into any of the ports in Cuba in distress, are subjected to the suspicions of the government, particularly if from Enemies ports, and although their distress be manifest, unnecessary and perplexing embarrassments are thrown in their way, and injurious delays occasioned. If the vessel thus situated has a Cargo, and is irreparable, or so much damaged that it becomes necessary to unload, and sell the Cargo, nearly the whole is sacrificed to sattisfy [sic] the duty, and pay the expence [sic] attending tedious and multifarious formalities.

12th  In every department of the Govt from the multiplicity of their injuries, and abuses upon them, frequent applications are required to be made by our citizens. The most abusive impositions are put upon them; their rights are regarded and business facilitated, only as they apply fees to clerks and officers, and they are treated with contempt, indifference, and ridicule.

13th  No American is allowed to transact his own business, in his own name, but must employ a Spanish subject to do it for him.

Innumerable minor impositions are imposed by minor officers of the Govt which I take no notice of, considering them as not directly authorized, though openly tolerated by the Govt. It is only those which originate with, or are publicly sanctioned by the chiefs of departments which I regard. Neither do I make any mention of the notoriously frequent and flagitious depradations [sic] upon our commerce within the jurisdiction of this Island, which are attended with sanguinary and barbarous treatment towards our citizens in almost every instance of capture, as it is my intention to make this the subject of some future remarks.

In this notice of the abuses on our commerce, although it is headed "Abuses &c in the Island of Cuba" I confine myself to Havana in my remarks thereon, because I cannot rely upon my information as it respects the other ports in the Island, and consider it a matter of small importance; their exports, and our trade with them being inconsiderable.

It becomes necessary however, for the information I wish to convey, to state, that the duty on flour given to the Count de Morpox of 1

25/100 Dollars is not exacted in those ports, his permission being granted for Havana alone.

. . .

But the Govt of Cuba have no sense of obligations, neither will they place our trade upon a just and reciprocal footing unless compelled to do it.

They pretend they have not the power; that they have not authority to reduce the duty; being bound by the laws, and instructions of their Court which forbid it. But this is not true. Although there may be laws affixing the duty, and instructions from the Court respecting neutral trade, the Govt and Intendent [sic] of the Island have discretionary power by other instructions to act as necessity shall dictate for its benefit and preservation. And there is no law respecting its trade, which under present circumstances they have not power to relax, revoke, or enforce, as they may deem convenient—

The following is the principle on which the excessive duty is exacted on goods imported in foreign Vessels. In Spain a duty of 15 pr Ct. on the valuation is exacted on entrance upon foreign goods, and seven pr Ct. on exportation to the colonies which makes 22 pr Ct. and on importation in the colonies a duty of 10 pr Ct. is exacted, which with half pr Ct. consulado duty makes 32½ pr Ct. It is necessary here to observe that most goods have a valuation fixed by law; but those that have not are estimated at the Custom House according to the then prices of the market—upon which valuation 8 pr Ct. is added before the calculation of duty is made—And that besides the 32½ pr Ct. There is a tax called vestuario for militia cloathing payable on all kinds of wine & spirits, at the rate of ⅜th of a Dollar for 4½ arrobas of the liquor. The barril de cargo of 6 to a pipe is reckoned at 4½ arrobas. The canary pipe at 30 arrobas—The pipe of Catalonia at 32 arrobas. Pipes of the other parts of Spain at 28 arrobas, & all other casks proportionately. Flour also pays a de vestuario duty of 3 reals or 37½ cts pr Barril. These are the duties affixed by the laws of Spain on goods of foreign growth or manufacture imported to Spain and exported from thence to the colonies. As these laws, nor any other ever contemplated the admission of foreign goods in the colonies direct from a foreign country, no provision was ever made for such cases. For this reason, I do not conceive this Govt have a right by law to exact more than 10½ pr Ct. on goods imported here in Am. Vessels. The opperation [sic] of the law is very different in its effects, whether goods are imported here by the circuitous rout[e] of Spain, or direct from a foreign Country. For instance—suppose goods to be shipped from the United States for Spain, the shipper on entrance there pays 15 pr Ct. The person who purchases them, exports them to Havana on paying 7 pr Ct. where on entrance they pay 10½ pr Ct. more; which being moderate, if the market is not glutted falls upon the consumer. Thus the duty is proportioned among them. But on goods imported direct from the United States the whole falls upon the importer, as has been shown in the preceding observations.

. . .

As there is an imposition in calculating the duty, and it is purposely involved in mystery & obscurity, I will unravel it. The following is the method of calculating the duty—

All goods are valued in the Arancel, or book of rates, in reals of Vellon, whereof 20 to the hard Dollar.

Desired to know the duty payable at Havana on 12¼ Ct wt of soap, which is rated in the arancel or spanish book of rates @ 80 rs of Vellon pr. Ct wt (which is rated lower according to its value than any other articles) multiply the wt vizt. 12¼ C wt by 80 rs Vellon is 980 rs Vn. amnt of the valuation—980 rs Vellon make 521 reals of plate, being in the proportion to each other of 64 to 34; because the real of plate is equal to 64 maravedis vellon, and the real of vellon equal to 34 of the same maravedis.

521 rs plate being amnt of the rated value of the soap 41 do do. for colonials augmentation on said sum of 521 rs @ 8 pr Ct. is 562 rs of plate. 10 pr Ct. on said sum of 562 rs for colonial duty makes 56 rs of plate, whereof 10⅝ to the hard Dollar.

These reals of plate, are converted into equal number of colonial reals of 8 to the Dollar for payment of the duty.

This operation furnishes only the colonial part of the duty on said quantity of soap; the remaining part being found as follows—

980 rs Vellon being amnt of the rated value of said soap, makes 392 colonial reals of 8 to the hard Dollar because said hard Dollar is equal to 20 rs Vellon. Now 22 pr Ct (being the European duty) on said sum of 392 rs of Havana, makes 86 Havana reals. This sum of 86 rs together with the before mentioned one of 56 rs make the amnt of duty payable at Havana on said quantity of 12¼ C wt of soap, exclusive of the consulado; which is charged on the foregoing sum of 562 rs @ ½ pr Ct & amounts to 2½ rs of Havana money; which added to the fore-

going sum of 86 & 56. make the whole duty 144½ rs or $18.6/100 on said soap.

This tedious, complicated operation may be abridged, by charging the amnt of the article as valued in the Arancel with 37 pr Ct. the result whereof will be exactly the same as in the other method; for instance, 980 rs vellon being amnt of the rated value of the soap @ 37 pr Ct. produces 362½ rs vellon; which sum brought into Havana reals of 8 to the Dollar, at the rate of 20 rs Vellon to the hard dollar, makes exactly 144½ rs or $18.6/100. Therefore the duty though nominally 32½ pr Ct on the valuation is actually 37 pr Ct. occasioned by the difference of exchange between the reals of plate in which the colonial duty is calculated, and the Havana real. The former being converted into an equal number of the latter.

By the regulation of 28th of May, there is a diminution in the duty of the Arancel goods of 7¼ pr Ct. from what they were subject to before that period; which is occasioned by the reduction of the reals of plate into colonial reals, in the due proportion, of that part of the duty which is charged @ 22 pr Ct; whereas heretofore, the reals of plate were payable in an equal number of Colonial reals, as it still continues to be on the other part of the duty of 10½ pr Ct. as exemplified in the above calculation of the duty on 12¼ C wt of Soap—So that the duty exacted previous to this regulation was actually 44¼ pr Ct.

In the preceding notes of abuses No 1—I have said the duty is about 26 pr Ct on the cost & charges in the United States. It may be something more, or less. I made this calculation from the duty paid on several Cargoes, and averaged the amnt with the aggregate amount of invoices of the said Cargoes.

It was a long time before I could ascertain the principle of calculating the duties. It did not seem to be known even in the Custom House; and there are not three merchants in the city that understand it.

A veil of mystery was thrown over it as on every thing else relating to the system & policy of this Govt, which it requires time & perseverance to penetrate."

# Appendix III

## Some Notes on American Agents to Cuba, 1812-1831

Stephen Kingston was appointed March 24, 1812. He arrived at his post July 4th but was not permitted to stay and was again in the United States July 25th. John Mitchell was appointed December 4, 1811, arrived at Santiago March 13, 1812, but was not permitted to remain.

George P. Stevenson was appointed in 1817 upon the refusal of Alexander Hamilton.

Michael Hogan reached Havana by December 14, 1819.

John Warner acknowledged his appointment, March 17, 1821; he arrived in Havana April 30th. He was frequently away. Sometimes John Mountain acted for him as in the summer of 1821. In the summer of 1822, George N. Rolls was his vice commercial agent and when he died he was succeeded by Francis C. Black. When Warner left in the summer of 1824, Mountain acted for him a second time. When Warner returned for the last time in January, 1825, he dismissed Mountain and made T. M. Rodney his assistant.

Rodney arrived in Havana by December 19, 1825 and appointed F. M. Dimond as his assistant. Gray also acted for him occasionally.

Thomas Bolling Robertson was first chosen as special agent, December 7, 1825, but he declined, so after an interval Daniel Pope Cook was appointed March 12, 1827.

Vincent Gray had a stroke late in October, 1831, and died November 9th.

John Quincy Adams began the attempts to gain the Florida archives by sending Colonel James G. Forbes down, March 10, 1821. In March, 1822, a naval officer, Captain James Biddle, had no better success. In December, William McRee declined to go and in April, Thomas Randall was sent. His mission was broader as he was to protest against piracy and investigate the slave trade, but he got no nearer the archives than the rest. The matter was then permitted to rest until Jackson's moves.

# Appendix IV

## The Documentary Structure of Benson's
## Monstrous Guano Empire

The following sentences illustrate the process of the construction of this colossus and something of the confusion of the record.

Benson acquired Malden and Christmas by "discoverers'" deeds of March 29, 1856, from G. E. Netcher and May 11, 1857, from John and Harriet Stetson. Bonds were dated, December 29, 1859. Most of these papers are in Guano Islands, IV under Malden.

G. W. Benson to Cass, December 24, 1858, sends deed from William H. Wood of New Bedford who discovered Starbuck in 1845, dated December 24, 1858. G. W. Benson to Cass, December 27, 1858, sends deed from James F. Hammond of Newport, Rhode Island, who went to Washington Island in 1845, dated October 6, 1858. George W. Benson to Cass, January 11, 1859, encloses deed and affidavit from Luther J. Briggs declaring William Hamilton of New Bedford landed at Macauley Island, May 15, 1835; affidavit and deed dated January 10, 1859. George W. Benson to Cass, January 21, 1859, submits affidavit and deed of January 21, 1859, that John P. Payne of Providence discovered Gardner Island, December 29, 1842. William W. Taylor to Cass, February 10, 1859, submitted affidavit of discovery of forty-two named groups in the Caroline, Sydney and Washington group which he had deeded to G. W. Benson, February 7, 1859. Reference is made in the records to G. W. Benson to John Appleton, Assistant Secretary of State, April 28, 1859, which I have been unable to find; A. G. Benson to Cass, July 7, 1860 (under Enderbury, Guano Islands, III). Bonds for all of these islands were dated February 8, 1860, and sent to the State Department February 14, together with G. W. Benson's deed for all of these to the United States Guano Company, dated January 4, 1860, A. G. Benson to Appleton, February 9, 1860, Appleton to A. G. Benson, February 14, 1860, Dom Letters LI, 458, to G. W. Benson, February 15, 1860, *ibid.*, 463, Cass to Howell Cobb, February 25, 1860, *ibid.*, 486. Cobb acknowledged the receipt of the bond March 1, 1860, Guano Is. III, under Caroline. The papers for most of these are under Caroline in Guano Islands III. See also Washington in *ibid.*, V, and Enderbury *ibid.*, III.

233

# Bibliographical Notes
## Chapters 1 and 2

United States National Archives
  Papers of the Continental Congress
  Papers of the State Department
    Foreign Letters
    Domestic Letters
    Instructions to Ministers
    Instructions to Consuls
    Dispatches from Spain
    Notes from Spanish Legation
    Dispatches from Havana Consulate
    Dispatches from Santiago (Cuba) Consulate
    Miscellaneous Letters
Spanish Archives
  Archivo Histórico Nacional, Estado (Library of Congress Transcripts)
  Ministerio de Estado (Library of Congress Transcripts)
  Archivo General de Indias, Papeles Procedentes de la Cuba
    (Library of Congress Transcripts)
Philadelphia Custom House Records
Library of Congress
  Sylvanus Bourne MSS
Massachusetts Historical Society
  Timothy Pickering MSS
New York Historical Society
  John Stoughton Letter Book
Government Documents
  American State Papers, Commerce and Navigation
  Journal of the Continental Congress, 1774–1789
  Senate Executive Journal
  Statutes at Large of the United States of America, 1789–1873
Henry Adams, *History of the United States during the Administrations
  of Thomas Jefferson and James Madison,* New York, 1889–1891
José Martín Félix de Arrate, "Llave del Nuevo Mundo antemural de las
  Indias occidentales," *Los Tres Primeros Historiadores de la Isla
  de Cuba,* Havana, 1876

Samuel F. Bemis, *Pinckney's Treaty,* Baltimore, 1926

Charles Lyon Chandler, *Inter American Acquaintances,* Sewanee, 1917

"River Plate Voyages," *American Historical Review,* XXIII, 816-824

"U.S. Merchant Ships in the Rio de la Plata," *Hisp. Am. Hist. Rev.,* II, III, 26-54, 159-176

Charles E. Chapman, *History of the Cuban Republic,* New York 1927

Isaac J. Cox, "Pan American Policy of Jefferson and Wilkinson," *Miss. Valley Hist. Rev.,* I, 222-223

Margaret B. Downing, "Oliver Pollock," *Ill. Cath. Hist. Rev.,* II, 196-207

Dorothy Burne Goebel, "British Trade to the Spanish Colonies, 1796–1823," *American Historical Review,* XLIII, 288-320

Ramon Guerra y Sánchez, "Las Primeras Crisis Económicas de Cuba y sus Relaciones con el Comercio de los Estados Unidos," *Proceedings of the Second General Assembly of Pan American Institute of Geography and History held . . . October 14-19, 1935,* 452-467

Pedro J. Guiteras, *Historia de la Isla de Cuba,* New York, 1866

Horace Edwin Hayden, *Biographical Sketch of Oliver Pollock,* Harrisburg, 1883

James A. James, *Oliver Pollock,* New York, 1937

J. Franklin Jameson, "St. Eustatius in the American Revolution," *American Historical Review,* VIII, 685

Diego Luis Molinari, "Commercio de Indias . . . 1791–1809," *Documentos para la Historia Argentina,* VII, Buenos Aires, 1916

Roy F. Nichols, "Trade Relations and the Establishment of the United States Consulates in Spanish America, 1779–1809," *Hisp. Am. Hist. Rev.,* XIII, 289-313

"Cuban Commercial Regulations in 1805," *ibid.,* XVI, 213-219

Ellis P. Oberholtzer, *Robert Morris,* New York, 1903

Charles O. Paullin, *Navy of the American Revolution,* Chicago, 1906

Jacobo de la Pezuela, *Historia de la Isla de Cuba,* Madrid, 1878

Herminio Portell Vila, *Historia de Cuba, en sus relaciones con los Estados Unidos y España,* Havana, 1938–1941

Ramon de la Sagra, *Historia económica, politica y estadistica de la Isla de Cuba,* Havana, 1831

Francis Wharton, *Diplomatic Correspondence of the American Revolution,* Washington, 1889

Arthur P. Whitaker, *Spanish American Frontier, 1783–1795,* Boston, 1927

Augustus B. Woodward, *A Representation of the Case of Oliver Pollock*, Carlisle, 1806

Henry M. Wriston, *Executive Agents in American Foreign Relations*, Baltimore, 1929

J. F. Yela Utrilla, *España ante la Independencia de los Estados Unidos*, Madrid, 1925

# Chapters 3, 4, 5, and 8

The main source for the career of William Shaler is the large body of his papers and those of his brother, Nathaniel, now in the Historical Society of Pennsylvania. Samuel L. Knapp included a sketch of his life in his *Treasury of Knowledge* and his kinsman included some account of his exploits in his *Autobiography of Nathaniel Southgate Shaler*. Information regarding his ancestry and kindred is found in Andrew F. Warner, *One of the Warner Families in America* and John E. Stillwell, *The History of the Stillwell and . . . Allied Families*. Data were supplied me by Mrs. Kate Hammond Forgarty and Frank Farnsworth Starr by correspondence. The work of his close friend, Richard J. Cleveland, *Narrative of Voyages and Commercial Enterprises* and of the latter's son, Horace William Shaler Cleveland, *Voyages of a Merchant Navigator*, supply most of the account of the Chilean episode. An account written by Shaler appears in the *American Register* of 1808 in the form of a narrative entitled, "Journal of a Voyage between China and the North Western Coast of America made in 1804."

United States National Archives

  Papers of the State Department

    Special Agents

    Instructions to Consuls

    Dispatches from Spain

    Filibustering Expedition against Government of Spain

    Dispatches from Havana Consulate

    Havana Consulate Letter Books

    Florida Archives

    Diaries of Jeremy Robinson

    Appointments File

Archivo General y Publico, Mexico, D.F.
  *Historia, Oberaciones de Guerra, Salcedo*
  *Historia, Oberaciones de Guerra, Arredondo*
  *Historia, Oberaciones de Guerra, Notas Diplomáticas*
Library of Congress
  James Monroe MSS
Historical Society of Pennsylvania
  William Shaler MSS
Charles C. Adams, *Middletown Upper Houses*, Middletown, 1908
Hubert H. Bancroft, *History of California*, San Francisco, 1886
  *History of Mexico*, San Francisco, 1886
  *History of the North Mexican States and Texas*, San Francisco, 1889
John W. Barber, *Connecticut Historical Collections*, New Haven, 1836
R. H. Bonnycastle, *Spanish America*, Philadelphia, 1819
*Official Letter Book of W. C. C. Claiborne*, Dunbar Rowland, ed., Jackson, Mississippi, 1917
H. W. S. Cleveland, *Voyages of a Merchant Navigator*, New York, 1886
Richard J. Cleveland, *Narrative of Voyages and Commercial Enterprises*, Cambridge, 1842
Isaac Joslin Cox, "Monroe and the Early Mexican Revolutionary Agents," *Annual Report, American Historical Association*, 1911, I, 199-215
*West Florida Controversy*, Baltimore, 1918
William Derby, *Geographical Description of the State of Louisiana*, New York, 1817
Milton Dunn, "History of Natchitoches, Louisiana," *Louisiana Historical Quarterly*, III, 26-56
Timothy Flint, *Condensed Geography and History of the Western States*, Cincinnati, 1828
  *Recollections of the Last Ten Years*, Boston, 1826
Lorenzo de la Garza, *Dos Hermanos Héroes*, Ciudad Victoria, 1913
Alexander Gillespie, *Gleanings and Remarks*, Leeds, 1819
"Diary of José Bernardo Gutiérrez de Lara, 1811–1812," Elizabeth H. West, ed., *American Historical Review*, XXXIV, 55-77, 281-294
Alexandre de Humboldt, *Voyage aux Régions Équinoxiales du Nouveau Continent*, Paris, 1825
D. Hamilton Hurd, *History of Fairfield County, Connecticut*, Philadelphia, 1881
Samuel L. Knapp, *Treasury of Knowledge*, New York, 1833, 1839, 1850

*Papers of Mirabeau Buonaparte Lamar,* Charles A. Gulick, Jr., and Katherine Elliott, eds., Austin, Texas, 1921

Joseph B. Lockey, *Essays in Pan Americanism,* Berkeley, 1939 "The Florida Intrigues of José Alvarez de Toledo," *Florida Historical Society Quarterly,* XII, 145-178

W. F. McCaleb, "The First Period of the Gutiérrez-Magee Expedition," *Quarterly of the Texas State Historical Association,* IV, 218-229

Juan Ignacio Molina, *The Geographical, Natural and Civil History of Chile,* Middletown, Connecticut, 1808

Roy F. Nichols, "Willam Shaler, Early American Ambassador of Good Will," *Proceedings of the Second General Assembly of Pan American Institute of Geography and History, held . . . October 14-19, 1935,* 476-485

"William Shaler, New England Apostle of Rational Liberty," *New England Quarterly,* IX, 71-96

Jean Bory de Saint-Vincent, *Voyage dans les quatres principales iles des mers d'Afrique,* Paris, 1804

Eugenio Pereira Salas, *Barques norteamericanos en Chile a fines de la era colonial,* Universidad de Chile, 1936

*Autobiography of Nathaniel Southgate Shaler,* New York, 1909

[William Shaler], "Journal of a Voyage Between China and the North-Western Coast of America made in 1804," *American Register,* III, 137-175, (Philadelphia, 1808)

Reprinted with introduction by Lindley Bynum, Claremont, California, 1935.

John Sibley, "Louisiana," *American Register,* IV

W. B. Stevenson, *Historical and Descriptive Narrative of Twenty Years' Residence in South America,* London, 1825

John E. Stillwell, *History of . . . Stillwell and Appendix of Allied Families,* New York, 1931

Amos Stoddard, *Sketches Historical and Descriptive of Louisiana,* Philadelphia, 1812

*Two Hundredth Anniversary of the First Congregational Church of Haddam, Connecticut,* Haddam, 1902

Andrew F. Warner, *One of the Warner Families in America,* Hartford, 1892

Arthur P. Whitaker, *The United States and the Independence of Latin America, 1800–1830,* Baltimore, 1941

A. Curtis Wilgus, "Spanish American Patriot Activity along the Gulf

Coast of the United States, 1811–1812," *Louisiana Historical Quarterly*, XIII, 193-215, XIV, 182-203
Justin Winsor, *Narrative and Critical History of America*, Boston and New York, 1899
H. Yoakum, *History of Texas*, New York, 1856

# Chapters 6 and 7

United States National Archives
  Papers of the State Department
    Special Agents
    Ghent-American Commissioners
    Instructions to Consuls
    Mediterranean Negotiations
    Dispatches from Algiers
  Papers of the Navy Department
    Captains' Letters
Historical Society of Pennsylvania
  Josiah L. Johnston MSS
  William Shaler MSS
*American State Papers, Foreign Relations*
John Quincy Adams, *Memoirs*, Philadelphia, 1874
*Writings of John Quincy Adams*, Worthington C. Ford, ed., New York, 1913–1917
Gardner W. Allen, *Our Navy and the Barbary Corsairs*, Boston, 1905
*Early Proceedings of the American Philosophical Society*, Philadelphia, 1884
*Transactions of the American Philosophical Society*, n.s., II, 438-465, IV, 1-48, Philadelphia, 1825, 1834
"Papers of James A. Bayard," *Annual Report of the American Historical Association*, 1913, II
Gabriel Hanotaux et Alfred Martineau, *Histoire des Colonies Françaises*, Paris, 1930
Ray W. Irwin, *Diplomatic Relations of the United States with the Barbary Powers, 1776–1816*, Chapel Hill, 1931
"An Early Pan American Scheme," Joseph B. Lockey, ed., *Pacific Historical Review*, II, 439-447

Sir Harry Burrard Neale, *A reply to erroneous statements and unwarranted reflections in a publication entitled: "Sketches of Algiers"* by W. Shaler, American Consul General for that Regency, Malta, 1826

Roy F. Nichols, "Diplomacy in Barbary," *Pennsylvania Magazine of History and Biography,* LXXIV, 113-141

*Nouvelle Biographie Générale,* XV, 298, Paris, 1868

Charles O. Paullin, *Diplomatic Negotiations of American Naval Officers,* Baltimore, 1912

R. L. Playfair, *Scourge of Christendom,* London, 1884

"Journal of Jonathan Russell, 1818-1819," *Proceedings of Massachusetts Historical Society,* LI, 488-495

William Shaler, *Esquisse de l'état d'Alger, considéré sous les rapports politique, historique et civil; contenant au tableau statistique sur la géographie, la population, le gouvernement . . . les événemens politiques et récens de ce pays. Traduit de l'anglais et enriche de notes par M. X. Bianchi. Avec un plan d'Alger, du port, des fortifications, et d'une partie de la radé; dressé d'après les documens officiels et rectifié sur les lieux mêmes,* Paris, 1830

*Sketches of Algiers,* Boston, 1826

Louis B. Wright and Julia H. Macleod, *First Americans in North Africa,* Princeton, 1945

# Chapters 9, 10 and 11

United States National Archives

Over the years the State Department accumulated a great mass of papers on the guano question. A large number of them, though by no means all, were gathered together in a special series of volumes labelled "Guano Islands." However, there are still many of the papers in the regular archival series, Domestic Letters (the Secretaries' copies of out-letters) and Miscellaneous Letters (the in-letter files). These are in chronological sequence and are only partially indexed; the guano enthusiast must search them almost page by page. In the Guano volumes, the papers are grouped under the names of the various islands which are filed in somewhat alphabetical succession. The principal locations are:

Alta Vela ....................Guano Volume I
Cayo Verde ...................Guano Volume I
Aves ........................Guano Volume II
Baker .......................Guano Volume III
Caroline ....................Guano Volume III
Enderbury ...................Guano Volume III
French Frigate Shoal ...........Guano Volume III
Howland .....................Guano Volume III
Jarvis ......................Guano Volume IV
Johnston ....................Guano Volume IV
Lobos .......................Guano Volume IV
Madison .....................Guano Volume IV
Malden ......................Guano Volume IV
Mona and Monita .............Guano Volume V
Navassa .....................Guano Volume V
Phoenix .....................Guano Volume V
Sombrero ....................Guano Volume V
Swan ........................Guano Volume V
Washington ..................Guano Volume V

Other guano papers are in the following State Department Series:
    Instructions to Peru
    Dispatches from Peru
    Notes to Peruvian Legation
    Notes from Peruvian Legation
    Dispatches from Bolivia
    Instructions to Ecuador
    Dispatches from Ecuador
    Notes from Ecuadorian Legation
    Instructions to Venezuela
    Dispatches from Venezuela
    Domestic Letters
    Miscellaneous Letters
Papers of the Navy Department
    Secretaries' Files
    Office of Naval Operations
Library of Congress
    Jeremiah S. Black MSS
    William L. Marcy MSS
    Daniel Webster MSS

Massachusetts Historical Society
  Edward Everett MSS
New Hampshire Historical Society
  Daniel Webster MSS
University of Chicago
  Stephen A. Douglas MSS
Government Documents
  Executive Order of the President, June 29, 1926, 4467
  Executive Order of the President, December 29, 1934, 6935
  Annual Reports of the Secretary of the Interior
    1936, 27-28
    1939, 345
    1945, 268
    1946, 425
  United States Navy Department
  Information on the Trust Territory of the Pacific Islands trans-
  mitted to the Secretary General of the United Nations, Washing-
  ton, 1948
  Assistant Chief of Naval Operations (Island Government),
  Report to the United Nations on Guam, American Samoa, and other
  Island Possessions Administered by the Navy Department, July,
  1946
Congressional Documents
  23rd Congress, 2nd Session, House Ex. Doc. 105 (Ser. 273)
  31st Congress, 1st Session, Senate Ex. Doc. 58, 59 (Ser. 561)
  31st Congress, 1st Session, Senate Ex. Doc. 80 (Ser. 562)
  32nd Congress, 1st Session, Senate Ex. Doc. 109 (Ser. 621)
  33rd Congress, 1st Session, House Report 347 (Ser. 744)
  33rd Congress, 2nd Session, Senate Ex. Doc. 31 (Ser. 751)
  34th Congress, 3rd Session, Senate Ex. Doc. 25 (Ser. 879)
  34th Congress, 3rd Session, Senate Report 397 (Ser. 891)
  35th Congress, 1st Session, Senate Ex. Doc. 69 (Ser. 930)
  35th Congress, 1st Session, Senate Report 307 (Ser. 939)
  35th Congress, 2nd Session, Senate Ex. Doc. 25 (Ser. 981)
  36th Congress, 1st Session, Senate Ex. Doc. 37 (Ser. 1031)
  36th Congress, 2nd Session, Senate Ex. Doc. 10 (Ser. 1082)
  54th Congress, 1st Session, Senate Report 606 (Ser. 3364)
  Congressional Globe, 33rd Congress, 1st Session
  Congressional Globe, 34th Congress, 1st Session

Congressional Globe, 62nd Congress, 1st Session
Congressional Globe, 63rd Congress, 1st Session
Jones vs. United States, 137 U.S. Reports, 202-224
British Parliamentary Papers. Correspondence respecting the Guano
    Islands of Lobos de Tierra and Lobos de Fuera, 1842–1852, pre-
    sented to the House of Commons in pursuance of their address of
    May 14, 1852
Baltimore *Sun*
Boston *Advertiser*
Boston *Transcript*
Buffalo *Commercial Advertiser*
Portland, Maine, *Advertiser*
New York *Herald*
New York *Journal of Commerce*
New York *Times*
Washington *Star*
American Farmer, v. VI, 346, 3rd Ser.; v. IV, 236, 349
American Year Book, 1937, 217-218; 1938, 211-212; 1940, 239
"Diary of Edward Bates," Howard K. Beale, ed., *Annual Report of the
    American Historical Association*, 1930, IV
Charles Barronilhet, *Opusculo sobre el Huano*, Paris, 1857
William Beebe, *Galápagos-World's End*, New York, 1924
A. G. Benson, *Memorial to Congress of January 8, 1855*, New York,
    1855
Clement Biddle, "Some Pacific Islets appertaining to the United States,"
    *Bull. Geographical Society of Philadelphia*, XVI, 18-26
Benjamin Bock, "Anglo-American Rivalry for Pacific Islands," *Inter-
    national Quarterly*, II, 29-34
S. Whittemore Boggs, "American Contributions to Geographical Knowl-
    edge of the Central Pacific," *Geographical Review*, XXVIII, 177-192
Jean Ingram Brookes, *International Rivalry in the Pacific Islands,
    1800–1875*, Berkeley, 1941
Edwin H. Bryan, Jr., *American Polynesia and the Hawaiian Chain*,
    Honolulu, 1942
Hawthorne Daniel, *Islands of the Pacific*, New York, 1943
Ed. M. Douglas, "Boundaries, Areas, Geographic Centers and Altitudes
    of the United States and the Several Islands," Department of
    Interior, Geological Survey, *Bulletin 817*, 54
W. E. Dunn, *Peru*, Washington, 1925

Ernest Gruening, Memorandum to author

*Guano, A Treatise on the History, etc.*, Boston, 1860

G. H. Hackworth, *Digest of International Law*, I, 502-524, Washington, 1940-1944

J. D. Hague, "Phosphatic Guano Islands of the Pacific Ocean," *American Journal of Science and Arts*, September, 1862

Thomas C. Hart, "United States and Pacific Islands," *Annals of the American Academy of Political and Social Science*, #255, 115-123

James R. Hibbs, Chapters in the relations of Venezuela and the United States, 1865-1889, MSS Dissertation, University of Pennsylvania, 1941

William H. Hobbs, *Fortress Islands of the Pacific*, Ann Arbor, 1945

George Evelyn Hutchinson, "The Biogeochemistry of Vertebrate Excretion," *Bulletin of the American Museum of Natural History*, XCVI, New York, 1950.

David N. Leff, *Uncle Sam's Pacific Islets*, Stanford, 1940

John Bassett Moore, *Digest of International Law*, Washington, 1906, *History and Digest of International Arbitrations*, Washington, 1898

Robert C. Murphy, *Bird Islands of Peru*, New York, 1925

*Navassa Island Riot*, Baltimore, 1889

William A. Nicholas, "American Pathfinders in the Pacific," *National Geographic Magazine*, LXXXIX, 617-640

Roy F. Nichols, "Latn American Guano Diplomacy," *Modern Hispanic America*, A. Curtis Wilgus, ed., (Washington, 1933), 517-544

"Navassa, a Forgotten Acquisition," *American Historical Review*, XXXVIII, 505-510

James L. O'Sullivan, "Trust Territory of the Pacific, 1945-1949," *American Foreign Service Journal*, XXVI, 16-17, 44, 46, 48

*Pacific Guano Company, Its History, Its Products and Trades, Its Relation to Agriculture*, 1876

*Peruvian and Bolivian Guano*, London and Baltimore, 1844

*Phosphatic Guano from Sombrero Island, West Indies*, 1858

Earl S. Pomeroy, "American Policy respecting Marshalls, Carolines and Marianas, 1898-1941," *Pacific Historical Review*, XVII, 43-53

*Pacific Outpost*, Stanford, 1951

Julius W. Pratt, *America's Colonial Experiment*, New York, 1950

George R. Putnam, "An Important Guide for Shipping," *National Geographic Magazine*, XXXIV, 401

*Report to Stockholders of United States Guano Company*, 1859

Robert W. Robson, *Pacific Islands Handbook*, Sydney, 1950

Santiago Tavara, *Administracion del Huano*, Lima, 1856

William J. Taylor, "Investigations on the Rock Guano from the Islands of the Caribbean Sea," *Proceedings of the Academy of Natural Sciences*, March, 1857

James E. Teschemacher, *Essay on Guano*, Boston and New York, 1845

*Writings and Speeches of Daniel Webster*, Boston, 1903

Howell Walker, "Air Age Brings Life to Canton," *National Geographic Magazine*, CVII, 117-132.

John K. Wright, ed., *Atlas of the Historical Geography of the United States* by Charles O. Paullin, Washington and New York, 1932.

# Index

247